Artichokes & Grace

Artichokes & Grace

Getting to the *Heart* of Aging
With Our Aging Parents and Within Ourselves

Kristen Falde Smith, M.S.G.

10 9 8 7 6 5 4 3 2 1

Published by Smith Family Publishing House
Rossmoor, California, USA
Designs, cover art, and layout by Chelsea Buell 2017

ISBN 13: 978-0-692-87833-0

Library of Congress cataloging information forthcoming

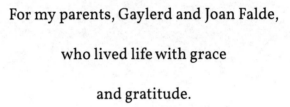

For my parents, Gaylerd and Joan Falde,

who lived life with grace

and gratitude.

I follow nature as the best guide and obey her like a god. Since she has carefully planned the other parts of the drama of life, it's unlikely that she would be a bad playwright and neglect the final act.

And this last act must take place, as surely as the fruits of trees and the earth must someday wither and fall. But a wise person knows this and accepts it with grace...

~Cicero (106-43 B.C.)

Contents

————

ACT II - *About Our Own Aging - As Told by Voices of Hope*

Prologue

— ♥ —

A Listen to Book

*W*hen did we get this old? This is a collective question that many of us over 50 years of age – and to some extent, people of earlier ages – are asking. As I ask myself this question, I think with some wonder and nostalgia: *It was only yesterday that I graduated from high school, or at least college. It was only yesterday that I was in my twenties and my parents were in their fifties. It was only yesterday that my kids were little and I worried about potty training and whether or not they would learn to read. It was only yesterday that I began a 40-year career in gerontology. It was only yesterday that I was still someone's daughter.*

The truth is that the yesterdays have added up. Here I am, in my sixties, semi-retired, children grown and out of the house, and both of my parents have died. Even though I still think of myself as "young-ish," it's an odd and sometimes unsettling feeling to stop and take stock of where I actually am in life – and I am guessing that it may be for you, too.

If you are anywhere near my age, you are one of the members of the famous baby boomer generation (born 1946-1964). The baby boomers are not one homogenous group of people, but a widely diverse cohort in almost every way. The one common denominator we have for certain is that we are all getting older.

Given that there are about 77 million of us, plenty of books have been written about *how to* live healthy longer, *how to* look younger, *how to* defy age altogether, *how to* appreciate wisdom and experience, *how to* find a second or third career, *how to* care for our aging parents (who are living longer), etc. – and there are a vast variety of products and resources to help us do all of these things. If you are a younger reader, you may be helping your mid-life parents deal with all of these issues.

However, in my experience, reading the *how to* books on aging – and I have read numerous ones – still leaves me with puzzling questions about the uneasy feelings I sometimes have about being in mid-life (for the purposes of this book, let's identify mid-life as 45 to 70). Questions such as, *How do we know that we have done our best in caring for our aging parents? How can we enjoy this journey of time when the years can bring unwanted change and loss? How do we let go of the past, especially past regrets, and live in the present with a spirit of gratitude? Or, on the lighter side, How can we find the humor in changing looks and slightly declining physical pursuits?*

To address these questions and many more, I conducted in-depth interviews with mid-life adults and asked them to share their stories about the two major acts that comprise the aging story – first, caring for aging parents and then second, crafting our own aging narrative. These acts are both part drama *and* part comedy. Aging definitely should be classified as *dramedy!*

The stories that are revealed as you travel through the conversations of this book are more than a *how to* instruction guide. They are a *listen to* experience that primarily focuses on positive aspects of the aging process, without diminishing the struggles. They are living stories with real voices.

In Act I, the mid-life adults, known as the Cast of "Character" (Cast), are our *Voices of Experience*. They share their joys, struggles, insights, reasons to laugh, and how it is that they are living grateful lives even as they have faced the challenges of being closely involved with their aging parents over many years. As you *listen to* their voices, you will be comforted to know that *you are not alone* in your journey with aging parents. You may discover new ways of thinking and coping from what they have to say. Above all, their voices will encourage you and inspire you to find joy in the caregiving process.

In Act II of our aging story, our Cast emerges as *Voices of Hope*. These same mid-life adults reflect on their own aging, partially in light of what they have experienced and learned from their aging parents, both positively and negatively. They also measure that knowledge with their own life's journey and offer insight and advice on how to navigate the passing of time and create an existence of purpose and meaning. They have learned what behaviors to discard and what behaviors to emulate. They have learned how to laugh at themselves. They have learned the true meaning of gratitude.

This is my wish for you, dear reader — that as you *listen to* the voices in this book, you will discover new ways to think and feel about the aging experience. I also wish for you that joy, laughter, gratitude and hope will become an integral part of your aging journey, with your parents and within yourself.

A Cast of "Character"

— 💙 —

"It occurred to me in the middle of the night,

this is not a Cast of Characters

but rather a Cast of 'Character.'"

~Kristen

I am pleased and excited to introduce the mid-life adults that I interviewed for this book. You will *listen to* their voices and discover that they are people of exceptional "character." They have dedicated countless amounts of time and boundless energy to providing their own unique form of care to aging parents.

They are not a random sample of the population, but rather people who were personally familiar to me or that I had heard of through friends and colleagues. I knew that parent care had been a top priority in their lives. Some had good relationships with their parents earlier in their lives, others did not. Some had strong family support with caregiving, others did not. Some had easy access to resources, others did not. Their common thread was, very simply, their distinctive dedication to their aging parents and their willingness to share their stories. These select individuals have partnered with me to present this aging dramedy. They are our Cast of "Character" [Cast].

In addition, these are people who I was quite certain would have given intentional thought to their own aging and, I believed, they would be willing to share that evolving perspective. As you will see, they have developed a vision of the present and the future that is a blend of what they learned from aging parents, their own unique personality and lifestyle, and an awareness of their changing place in the life cycle.

The one-hour interview that I had planned, without exception, transformed into a rich sharing and discussion that lasted well over two hours, sometimes three or four. I was honored to be the person recording these voices – and now sharing them with you – and I was overwhelmed by the deeply sensitive and personal information that these individuals were willing to reveal. I originally planned on having a much larger Cast. But with the depth of sharing and the willingness to cover difficult topics in the interviews, I opted for quality over quantity. It was the right decision.

These, then, are the voices of those who have walked alongside their aging parents on a rather long journey – with joy, sorrow, success, failure, laughter, tears, resentment and gratitude. If you listen carefully, you will gain knowledge, develop insight, and grab onto the courage and hope that you need to successfully navigate the journey with your aging parents. In addition, you will gather gems from their experiences as you are launched into the path of your own personal aging journey.

I gave each person of the main Cast the task to create an individual introduction. I requested a brief description of their role as caregiver to a parent and/or to state the meaning of the caregiving experience. The underlying question was what each person most wanted the reader to know. Here is who they are and what they said.

Main Cast

Dawn is the executive director of a multi-level retirement community. She has a gentle and sincere personality, and an ever-present calm and reassuring voice. Yet, Dawn remains firm when important values are at stake, and she leads her retirement community with an unquestionable dedication to her residents, family and staff. She is an only child; when her parents began to require some attention, Dawn translated that same level of dedication into meeting their needs.

"I was my parents' advisor, helping them in the decision-making process. I was their protector, their guide, and I oversaw their care. My dad allowed me to help them without making me feel bad."

Ellis is an educator and consultant in gerontology and organizational development. Ellis is crazy creative! She can come up with more ideas in 10 minutes than I can in 10 days! And she follows through on many of them. Ellis is vibrant, hilarious, and she brings these characteristics to her teaching of seniors and gerontology students. Needless to say, she is a very popular teacher. Ellis says that she was raised to believe that she could do anything, and she adores and thanks her parents for instilling within her this sense of passion for life.

"Caregiving is a privilege, and even though I thought I knew what to do, I fumbled, lost my patience, was upset with my father and siblings, and made all the mistakes that most caregivers do. In the end though, I knew it was all right ... I did my best. I loved, absolutely loved the person my mother was, and I miss her every day ... Caregiving is the hardest job I have taken on, but it was also one of the most satisfying."

Kathi has lived alone all of her adult life. She is an office executive for a major metropolitan opera company. Responsible, capable, and patient when working through difficult situations at work and at home describe her well. But in addition, she has a sense of adventure and will travel the world on her own and take on volunteer projects for church and community groups that are completely outside of her specific expertise. Kathi says that someone has to do it and she always gets the job done.

"My dad checked into Cedars-Sinai on St. Patrick's Day, 2005, to have throat surgery to remove polyps from his vocal cords, an event which changed our family's course forever. The surgery left him unable to swallow food. He had to have a surgically inserted feeding tube. During the last six and a half years, my ordinary role as a middle age, unmarried daughter and friend to my parents has expanded to a multi-task role as chauffeur, TV companion, counselor, financial assistant, and Mom's chef. To be clear on the last point: I do not cook, but I know where the finest prepared foods can be bought."

Mike is a highly successful real estate developer. He is definitely the surprise member of my Cast. I only was familiar with him through other friends and would see him at large parties. On the surface, Mike seemed like a good-time guy, always funny, always telling stories. Hmm ... probably not a candidate for an interview on aging.

Then one evening my husband and I sat across the aisle from Mike and his wife at a small restaurant in our community. We started with the usual small talk before ordering food and moving on with our separate dinners, and suddenly Mike started talking about his parents. We sat and listened as he shared with such caring and such sadness about his dad's death and his mother's current health struggles. I discovered this wonderful internal strength of character and passion. I asked him for an interview. He said yes.

"Helping my parents with doctors, hospitals, hospice care, and their last moments of life was both an honor and great source of pride for me. I know my brothers and sister felt the same. We were able to repay them, so to speak, for all the care and love they gave each of us for so many years."

Patsy is a social worker and an executive for a large city in Southern California. A highly intelligent professional with the ability to prioritize and accomplish a multitude of important tasks in her long day, she still manages to carve out time for family, friends, and fun. I think she just doesn't sleep. Patsy also approaches life as a continuous learning experience, looking for new ways to approach problems, develop fresh ideas, and never settle for the status quo. As a bonus, she also has a wonderful sense of humor!

"As the only one of my siblings living nearby, I gradually became my mother's bookkeeper, health care advocate, appointment scheduler and all-around problem-solver. I was her protector and supporter, providing reassurance along with options when previously simple tasks became impossible or unsafe for her."

Peter is the baby of the Cast. He is a composer and the owner of a studio-music contracting business. He has had a lot on his plate at a fairly young age, with both work demands and parent demands. Although he can still be wonderfully child-like and in awe of the world around him, Peter also carries an anxiety with him that is sometimes overwhelming. But his religious beliefs allow him, when he is especially burdened, to give his worries over to God. Then he is able to move forward and tackle a problem with renewed energy and hope.

"Being a caregiver for my mom broke down our walls of frustrations with each other. She had been difficult to be close to, and this experience healed us in a way I never expected could ever happen."

Terry is the pragmatic, completely down-to-earth member of our Cast. He is a corporate executive for a large not-for-profit senior housing, health, and services organization. He is deliberate in his actions, and wants to always be able to measure results, no matter how abstract the issue may be. Terry has an amazing ability to listen to many different opinions, and then clarify how the group should proceed to the next step. What he says is always, sometimes annoyingly, logical.

"I am able to use my over 30 years of experience in the aging field to monitor my parents' well-being, even though they live at a great distance. I advise my parents and siblings on how to meet their individual needs today and what might arise in the future."

Supporting Cast

Deep into the writing of this book, I did realize that there were some gaps, some missing pieces. Simultaneously, I would run into people who had stories about their parents that would almost miraculously fill these gaps. I am absolutely not a "this is meant to be" person, but listen to this.

I had decided that I needed more story-based information on Alzheimer's disease – this was actually after I thought I had finished writing this book. Coinciding with this decision, I kept running into a woman at the grocery store that I really hadn't seen much in years. Every time we would meet, always in the produce section, she would give me an update about her mother who is suffering from Alzheimer's. **Diana** and her mother became one of my stories.

About the same time, I ran into a high-school friend at the JFK airport in New York. We both live in California. A few weeks later when I was scouring my brain to come up with one more Alzheimer's story, **Tom** popped into my mind. I remembered that at our 40th high school reunion, which had been a few years prior to the JFK encounter, he had talked about his mother having Alzheimer's. I gathered up my courage, called him, and asked if I could interview him about his Alzheimer's journey with his mother. He said, "It would be an honor."

Friends and colleagues who read my rough draft told me to strengthen the first chapter, the "Joy" chapter. Shortly after receiving this worrisome input, I had a wonderful conversation at book club with **Alyce** about her mother, and knew that she could add an important perspective about joy. Within this same time period, in conversation with my close friend **Geri**, she started talking about creating "joy moments" with her mother. I laughed out loud! This was exactly what I needed to give the final touch to that challenging chapter on Joy!

And then there is **Joann**. She is the wife of one of my husband's colleagues. We were on a company trip together and spent an afternoon bobbing around in the pool. As we bobbed up and down, she told me about experiences with her mother that were happy, sad, funny, frustrating, inspiring – everything you would expect. I have woven her stories into the narrative of this book in a variety of places.

Here is a brief description of the supporting cast. You will hear their telling quotes within their specific stories

Alyce was a stay-at-home mom for five children, and is now a stay-at-home caregiver for her 97-year-old mother. She is gentle, kind, and radiates warmth.

Diana is an independent accountant working for several small businesses. She is straightforward and practical, attending to every detail with her mother. Her top priority is to assure all aspects of her mother's dignity.

Geri is a highly successful professional musician. She has become the Italian matriarch for her family and completely relishes her role as caregiver, creator of "joy moments," coordinator of all medical issues for both parents, and surrogate mother to her siblings.

Joann, my pool-bobbing buddy, has very recently become a phlebotomist, and she is working at a hospital in the research department for first-time pregnant moms. She is delighted to be starting in a new career, even as she continues to be the primary support for her mom. She is gregarious and always eager for adventure.

Tom is an attorney who owns his own law practice. He possesses a genuine spirit of warmth and caring. He is the rock of his family, the person that his mother and his siblings look to for support.

The Last Cast Member

I am the narrator who had the privilege of conducting the interviews with this extraordinary group of people. I am also a "voice" – a character in our Cast – throughout the book, sharing some of my own personal stories and insights. I will also intermittently provide relevant professional information that I have compiled through the course of a 40-year career in the field of gerontology.

When I first started my work in gerontology, many of my friends didn't understand why I had chosen this field. They thought it was depressing, negative, and focused on death and dying. It is actually true that before my first day of work, my boss did require me to read *On Death and Dying* by Elisabeth Kubler Ross, which turned out not to be a depressing book at all, but actually very inspiring. After just a few weeks on the job, I discovered at the young age of 23, that I had a gift for relating to older people. I loved their stories. I loved how much they appreciated what I did for them. I loved how much they were willing to accept me. I loved them.

And I discovered the joy of helping people close out their lives – maybe for years or months or only a few days. Sad? Very. But rewarding beyond measure! So, with a mixture of years of experience and a passion for making the older years meaningful, I will take you on this journey of discovery about finding joy in caring for aging parents and in growing older ourselves.

A Final Note

In the first chapter, I will reintroduce the main Cast by their profession. For the remainder of the book, I will only refer to them by name. I hope you will use the descriptions here to refer back to when you want a reminder of a more personal description.

ACT I

About Aging Parents

As Told by

Voices of Experience

Introduction to Act I

Defining Moments

*I*t was Christmas Eve, and my family was sitting at the dinner table in my parents' dining room. We were delighting in our holiday Norwegian feast of *lutefisk*, *lefse* and meatballs. Toward the end of the meal, my dad said that he had something "just a little troubling" to tell us. We all paused and put our forks down. We looked at him expectantly and somewhat nervously. He said that he had found some blood in his urine and that he would be going in to the doctor's office for some tests. Since it was Christmas time, he was going to wait for a few weeks. He reassured us that the doctor thought that the blood was probably due to a urinary tract infection. The year was 1988. My dad died in 1989 of an aggressive form of prostate cancer that occurs in only 20% of men with this diagnosis.

Several years later, I spent a long, exhausting morning shopping with my mother at Macy's department store. She had called the night before to tell me that she had a coupon for 25% off of everything in the store. She wanted me to shop with her for a new dress. Although she tried on several dresses over a few hours time, we were unsuccessful in finding something that fit her well. We stopped for lunch. As we were eating, she said to me, "Let's go to Macy's. I've got a coupon for 25% off of everything in the store, and I want to buy a new dress."

Less than a year later, my mother was diagnosed with "probable" Alzheimer's disease.

I remember these specific moments just as I remember where I was when JFK was assassinated and what I was doing when I heard the news about the World Trade Center attack. These are moments, *defining moments,* when you suddenly realize, with a feeling of dread and uncertainty, that something has changed, something is shifting. Some defining moments change the world – and some defining moments change our own personal world.

When our own personal world begins to change, as the shifting of parent/child roles sneaks up on us, we anxiously realize that we are in unfamiliar territory. We have many questions, but few answers. We may feel very alone. We may be the first in our peer group to experience parent-related changes. Or maybe we haven't had time to pay much attention to the changing personal worlds of our friends.

So we embark on a journey with our aging parents that is tough to navigate, that will require us to build a reservoir of knowledge, that will have numerous potholes and detours. We will also discover our strengths and coping mechanisms that help us provide meaningful care to our aging parents. Ultimately, this journey will bring us the reward of knowing that we have gone the distance, and within our own personal world, we have done our best.

Aging Parent Talk Is Everywhere

Some years ago my husband and I attended a weeklong event in Maui. His finance company hosts the event for very successful car dealers, who have met multiple criteria to win this very nice trip. We've been on similar trips for many years now. The tone and location of these events promote fun, relaxation, light conversation – very little business, although some business talk does crop up over dinner and drinks. There is always something to say about the company, the economy or the government, no matter how beautiful the setting!

This trip I experienced something different. I found myself, over and over again, not in the small talk conversations that are usually the main fare, but in conversations with dealers and/or their spouses about their parents – *their aging parents.* At a lovely dinner one night, I asked the woman next to me what was going on in her life, expecting to hear about her kids, and she said, "Parent care." We proceeded to have a lengthy discussion of all of the dynamics going on in her family related to the challenges of taking care of aging parents.

One morning, I was involved in a catamaran/snorkeling activity. Another participant (a woman who is the CEO of a company that owns multiple automobile franchises) said, "I have to call my mother and tell her that I am finally in the water. She keeps asking if I have been in the water yet. I call her every day." When I favorably remarked on her strong connection to her mother, she told me that her mom lives alone in Florida. The daily phone calls are a subtle way of making sure that her mother is doing all right and also provide her with important social interaction. I was impressed that someone as busy as this CEO would include her mother in her daily schedule!

The next day, I went out to lunch with the wife of one of my husband's colleagues, who is a retired attorney. The two of us wanted to have a nice quiet lunch, without having to mingle with the dealer group. We spent almost the entire time talking about the difficulties that had surrounded her father's illness and death. Aging parent talk *was* everywhere!

For better or for worse – I contend mostly for better – adult children are often spending many years in the company of their aging parents, and are, in some manner, sharing the job with parents of navigating their advancing years. As a result, I seem to encounter aging parent talk wherever I go – not just during my vacations! I ran into an acquaintance that I hadn't seen in years at the grocery store. What did we talk about? Her mother's struggle with Alzheimer's disease. My daughter and I were having a leisurely cup of coffee at an outdoor café, and we saw a mother/daughter duo that we know. What did we talk about? The variety of serious health issues that are forcing a change in the living situation of the in-laws/grandparents. I go to my book club – what do we talk about? The book, some, of course, but we always get into aging parent conversations. One club member has her 95-year-old mother living with her. Another has recently lost her father. We all have a story.

Sharing Our Stories Is Essential

Sharing stories – the core premise for this book – is a very effective way to discover good approaches and helpful resources. Whether it's during a trip to Maui or shopping at the local grocery store, the sharing of stories illustrates the truth that millions of us are on the same chapter of our lives, and we are definitely not the only character in the book. This current life chapter on aging parents in which we find ourselves presents challenges, difficulties and sorrows related to age, to the passing of time. But this same chapter in life also has the potential to strengthen our experience of joy, laughter, gratitude and hope – within our parents' lives, and within our own.

The power of stories as a tool for learning has been a dominant theme in my professional and personal life. As a young gerontologist in my twenties, I had read and studied about the many theories of aging, analyzed policies that affected older people, and generally had good book knowledge on the subject of aging. It was only as I began to *listen to* the stories of the residents in my retirement community that I became excited about the prospect of a life-long career in gerontology.

In my job, I was fortunate to be in the position of listening to people's stories quite frequently. An adult child and aging parent would share the circumstances that had brought them to visit the retirement community. The stories were so often about their shared efforts for the parent to stay at home and then the recognition that it was probably not the best solution. I would listen and marvel at the sincerity and authenticity of their struggles in decision-making that led them to my door. The stories, though usually fraught with fear of change, became uplifting as the intimate connection between aging parent and adult child unfolded. I recognized that these stories enriched both the storyteller and the listener. The idea of writing a book about important themes in aging through people's voices began to simmer in my thinking.

On a personal level, as the years passed, my conversations with friends increasingly shifted from what our children were doing to what our parents were doing. In my particular group of friends, I was the first to experience sadness and loss with my parents. I found that I had something very special to offer by sharing the struggles and the triumphs of my journey with them. And it helped me immensely to tell my story – maybe even more so than it helped the person listening. It helped me get past some of the sorrow and recognize how much I contributed to my parents' lives in their final years, months, days and moments.

I

Caring for Aging Parents - Choose Joy

— 🖤 —

"Do it right and finish well."

~Peter

*J*oy is a choice when providing care to aging parents. It may be an easy choice for you or you may have to dig deep and be persistent to find it.

In our busy, scattered lives of today, the challenges of parent care may feel like a huge burden. There are too many things to do, and taking care of parents seems like a negative and overwhelming proposition. Contrary to this perspective, the adult children that I interviewed – our Cast of "Character," (Cast) - share that parent care can be a joyful and rewarding experience. It can be an experience for which to be grateful, one that can add richness to otherwise harried lives.

Joy will definitely not always be the natural reaction as we navigate the ups and downs that come with our parents' advancing years. As we will explore in Act I of this book, there is sorrow, there are obstacles, and there is grief. Sometimes, there is resentment and conflict too. All normal. All understandable. All part of the human experience.

The decision to choose joy reminds me of laboriously working my way through eating my favorite vegetable — an outwardly prickly, grainy artichoke — leaf by leaf, small bite by small bite. I am choosing to eat this artichoke, despite its difficulty. I have to avoid the sharp tips unless I have painstakingly cut them off. The outer leaves are usually rather tough but I carefully eat the very edge, getting just a hint of tasty goodness. As I get to the inner softer leaves, I begin to remember why I love this artichoke. I bite into the tender meat, yielding more flavor and more enjoyment with every layer. When the leaves are gone, I still have work to do. I must gently carve out the "furry stuff" to finish eating my vegetable. Then, eventually, with patience, I discover the delicious, tender *heart*. A well-placed drip of butter and that is one delicious morsel of joy, a source of great pleasure! The destination is definitely worth the journey!

Just like my artichoke, so it is with our aging parents. We have to patiently search for those morsels of joy. Because when we find them, and remember them, even though they are sometimes buried deep inside, they can carry us, and our parents, through otherwise trying times. This is why a discussion of joy must be our first consideration in this *dramedy* about aging.

As you *listen to* our Cast share their stories and identify many reasons for finding joy, sometimes in surprising or extraordinary places, I hope you begin to discover how to find your own joy within the unfolding experience of caring for your parents.

Positive Payback

When our parents begin to need our assistance, it can be helpful to first intentionally remember all that they have done for us to start building a positive foundation. We need to constantly build on this positive foundation so that we can gather strength when providing care gets difficult. Our parents weren't perfect, we probably didn't always agree with their point of view, and we certainly didn't want to follow their rules. But those days are gone and we need to draw on our ability to recognize the sacrifice that it takes to be a parent — the time, the money, the emotional investment. Isn't it our turn to be there for them — to give back to them for all that we have received? Our Cast says, "Yes!"

"It was my chance to give back to them – I owed them so much," expresses Dawn, who in the midst of a very demanding job as administrator of a multi-level care retirement community, shopped for her parents, visited them regularly, and was an integral part of their end-of-life care. *"I was an only child, their 'wonderful miracle,' and they had given me all of their love and attention."*

Not all adult children can claim to have been the "miracle child," though. Mike was more of a challenge for his parents as they raised him. This highly successful real estate developer shares, *"The greatest joy was the fact that I could take care of my parents financially – and it helped me personally to take care of them. I felt like I was paying them back for being such a horrible son. I was the problem child who discovered beer at 15 and girls at 16."* Mike laughs as he goes on to tell of talking his parents into allowing him to go to an all-night party, only to get in trouble so that they had to come and get him out of jail later that night. Definitely not the miracle child, at least not then. *"So taking care of my parents was a joy – they were wonderful and forgiving parents."*

Terry, a corporate health care executive, has the additional complication of providing care at a geographic distance. Still, he is also positive. *"Helping to take care of my parents is an opportunity to do for them and that feels good,"* he shares. *"It is also a joy, knowing that helping to care for them is the help that they need. They are having a better life as a result."*

Being in the Present

"Totally in the moment!" That's how Ellis, an educator and consultant in gerontology and organizational development, describes the time she spends with her aging parents. *"My mom and dad laugh a lot,"* says Ellis. *"They are amusing in how they see life. They don't take things too seriously and remind me that 'this too shall pass.' I marvel at their ability to find joy in life even though there is a great deal of sadness. I realize that it takes a special person to not be bitter about the losses of age."*

When Ellis speaks about her parents, her eyes beam with love, and her voice is strong and animated. *"My respect for them goes so deep when I take the time to listen. Sometimes I have to physically slow down and take a deep breath. Then I realize that I will not always have those moments of listening and laughing."* She recognizes how special these moments are – they will not last forever and she cherishes them.

Our caregiving role for our parents almost mandates that we live in the moment. We don't know how long or short the journey will be. When we find the good, the humor, the warmth of each small interaction and really pay attention, it gives us an experience with our parents that adds depth to an ever-evolving relationship.

Renewed Family Closeness

Over the years, families often become separated, either by geography and/or by diverse interests. Parent care can build a bridge that brings family members together again. It can be a newfound common interest and ideally requires a team effort. Based on the interviews with our Cast, we will look at the positive aspects, the joy aspects, of family dynamics that underlie a parent's need for assistance. If you are dealing with a negative or difficult family member, you might want to highlight these more uplifting possibilities for inspiration amidst your struggles.

Patsy, an executive for a large city in Southern California says, *"I learned more about my siblings, what their values were. I developed a new closeness with them,"* Patsy shares. *"Also, I like to learn, so there was a certain joy in learning about the issues related to her care and being able to share new information with my family. Many of my mom's friends were very kind, caring, and came forward to help—they were like family. I realized that a lot of people really loved my mom. As she needed more care than what our family could provide, we worked together to find some wonderful care places and wonderful caring people."* Patsy's comments underscore that caregiving can be a time for reflection, learning, and renewed closeness. For her, these are reasons for joy.

Renewed closeness of family has also brought joy for Kathi, an office executive for a major metropolitan opera company. *"I am truly spending more time with my family now that my dad needs care. We could go for weeks, in the past, without seeing each other or even talking on the phone. Our lives were busy. Now I spend so much more time with them, and I know that I won't have any regrets, wishing that I had spent more time with my family and my parents."*

She pauses and then continues, *"My sister and I have more consciously begun to meld our relationship. We are very different and now this is a time to close ranks. We never spent time together before and now we see the importance of family – it's a good thing. This whole thing of my parents needing some care and attention is bringing my family together. We take time for celebrations, birthdays our family has a new lease on life."*

Mike shares a similar feeling. *"When my father was a surgeon,"* he says, *"he didn't have time to spend with his family. With aging and illness, there was time for us to spend together."*

A New Perspective of Our Parents

The transition into life's later stages often requires our parents to adopt a new pace that suits their changing interests and possibly changing abilities. This creates an opportunity for you as adult children to gain a new appreciation of your parent's internal strength. For Patsy, it was the marvel of her mother's whole new career.

In Patsy's experience, there was a lengthy period when her mother was ill and needed care from family. During that time, she reflected about her mother. She marveled at how her mom had successfully negotiated 18 years as a single senior woman. After Patsy's father died, her mother developed a *"whole second life. She became a real estate agent, went to many activities, had many friends ... she was able to successfully make a transition and developed her own circle of close people. It was joyous to focus on how she was able to develop a whole new life after her mate died."*

Sometimes, it can just be a new insight from conversations that we now make time to have. I specifically remember sitting with my mom, a few years after my dad died, and I suddenly had a need to ask her about her hopes and dreams. She had always worked inside the home raising my three siblings and me. I didn't know anything about what other aspirations she might have had. I never took the time to ask her. So I asked Mom what she would like to have done if she hadn't been a full-time mother, and her answer astounded me! I expected her to say something along the lines of always wanting to be a wife and mother, even though she did have a college degree. Instead, my mother said, *"I would like to have been a test cook in the Betty Crocker Kitchen or an interpreter at the United Nations. I was always really good at languages."* It was an answer that gave me a whole new perspective about my mother! I believe she was completely happy in the life that she shared with my dad. However, I was enormously pleased to find out that she also had other ambitions and abilities. Look for these moments, these conversations . . . they can form an important part of the positive foundation for your journey.

Healing Relationships

Taking care of a parent inherently has an intimate quality that may feel challenging for the adult child and/or parent especially if a close intimacy didn't previously exist in the relationship. This intimacy may initially be a source of embarrassment or even humiliation. It will likely take an act of courage combined with a humble heart to embrace this intimacy and allow it to mend past hurts and disappointments.

Peter, a composer and studio contractor, found joy rather than sadness in his mother's vulnerability. *"She was in a place of letting down her guard, and she was able to let us love her. She was always strong and strong-willed . . . In her fear and frailty she was able to reach out to us. That brought a lot of healing. She was finally able to tell me that she loved me."* Over many years, Peter's family relationships were tense and distant. With his mother's illness, there was *"a lot of reuniting going on,"* notes Peter. *"We were able to recall good memories and did a lot of reminiscing as a family."*

Peter now understands himself better through providing care to a mother who had been difficult and unreasonably demanding. He was able to get in touch with some of his physical and emotional challenges, which were similar to hers. *"In some kind of an odd way,"* he says, *"there was a revelation – we are part of the same cloth. And I had to grow up a lot – I had to go from being her son to being a man. It was kind of a 'transferring of the deed.'"*

Stories of Creating "Joy Moments"

Geri is Italian. She believes in family without question. Over the past years, her mother has developed Alzheimer's disease, and she is now in advanced stages, living in a care facility. Her father, a legendary musician, is going "straight ahead" with gusto at 91 years old. Geri talks about the unique challenges for the family to create joy moments. She says, *"I found it a challenge to not be resigned to this decline in life for both of my parents. So my mission was 'how can we get through this so we can still create happy memories even in this very last chapter that is laden with sadness.' I tried to find the lemonade in the lemons and create situations that might bring joy to not only Mom and Dad, but to me!"*

Geri continues, *"While Mom was home, it was very difficult because Dad didn't understand her disease. He was critical of her and then she would explode. I tried to remember the things she used to like and do them with her, even though our past relationship was not spent hanging out together. The different phases of her Alzheimer's lent themselves to different ways to spend time together."*

Here is a sample of Geri's "joy moments with Mom." These moments did not simply emerge. Geri made them happen, she created them, and she chose them. They will hopefully inspire you to find your own unique moments of joy with your aging parents.

Joy moments when her mother was still living with her husband in her own home:

- **Lunch in the backyard.** *"We would set up a little bistro table and just sit out on the grass and have a soiree!"*

- **"Kidnapping" her ("to get her away from my dad").** *"I would take Mom out to get ice cream. I'd enthusiastically say: 'Come on. Let's go!' Then off we went to Baskin Robbins, and we'd come home and make colorful waffle cones."*

- **Rides in the convertible.** *"I have a convertible car. I would pick my mother up, take her on a drive with the top down through the Santa Monica Mountains, and continue on out to the beach. Mom didn't marvel at nature as I thought, but I did, and it felt good to be alone with her in this way."*

- **Exercise.** *"I took her for a walk along Ventura Boulevard* [a street with shops and restaurants in Los Angeles] *and went window shopping."*

- **Sensory stimulation.** *"We went to the Amazon Restaurant because it has huge waterfalls inside, and the restaurant is decorated with hanging birds and walls crawling with plants. She loved the beauty in there."*

- **Relaxation.** *"When she would visit me and be impatient with her grandkids, I had her sit at the edge of my pool with her feet in the water and play with a Frisbee, moving around the water's edge. She would become peaceful."*

- **Familiar Activities.** *"Let's make meatballs!! She used to love to cook."*

- **Dress up!** *"She was always a fashionista, so why not now? We would play with hats and scarves."*

- **Never too late to tap dance!!** *"She loved tapping as a kid and young adult. She had a pair of tap shoes that fit, so we put them on and she was so excited! She was laughing and thinking she couldn't do it but she went to town. I got this on video."*

- **Appreciating great music.** *"She always loved the pianist Vladimir Horowitz so I would play his VHS tapes on TV. She'd lie on the couch moving her arms in the air as if she were conducting with such love of the music. Sometimes she would bolt up, sitting straight up and passionately say,* 'That is SO BEAUTIFUL!!' *and then lay down again."*

- **Making her laugh!** *"America's Funniest Home Videos is a hands-down winner for all of us – like a magic pill. My siblings would say it is so difficult visiting her because she is so frustrated.* 'Put on the DVD!' *Then she would belly laugh. She loved the kids and animals."*

- **Memories.** *"We played videotapes of Italy. My brother would speak Italian to her and call her 'principessa,' the princess. The movie,* Life is Beautiful, *has an opening scene that would make her laugh. It gave us joy to see her reaction to it."*

Joy moments in the assisted living community:

- **A touch of nature.** *"As she declined, the joy was there, I just had to go deeper. I would look deep into her eyes and there was the twinkle. I would take her outside in her wheelchair to just look at the backyard fruit trees. I would walk around the yard pointing them out, and her eyes followed me and she would nod as I explained what they were. Her face was lit with joy at being outside."*

- **Music as therapy.** *"I love playing my flute for her. She always loved music and we used to play flute and piano together. I play for her standing right in front of her and our eyes lock. It is the most intimate connection we have ever had. I play a piece and then hug and kiss her, play another and do the same. Very, very healing and meaningful for me."*

Geri's "joy moments with Dad" are a completely different experience. Her father exemplifies fierce independence. Combined with that independence, though, is the demanding and often inflexible dad who exhorts them to always move "straight ahead." There is no time for emotion, for understanding, for accepting of life's difficulties. Just go forward! As Geri states, *"He sucks all of the life out of us* [his children] *so that he can go straight ahead."*

At the same time, Geri deeply loves her father, and she admires his powerful spirit. She is also devoted to creating "joy moments" with her strong Italian father.

- **Becoming a medical advocate.** *"It gives me great joy to spare him of questionable surgeries. I know I have saved his life and quality of it, due to many interventions and a hawk-like attitude about what is necessary and what is not."*

- **Reminiscing on the road.** *"After he had a stent put in at 91 years old, he couldn't drive for two weeks. That put the 'burden' on me of driving him around – 150 miles every other day! He went to see my mom every other day, and her care facility is 30 miles from his home. My home is near her, so the route was my house to his, take him to church, take him to the donut store, take him to Mom's,* *and then back to his and then back to mine! 150 miles! Burden? No! He loves music and would bring his CDs and share his favorites with me, telling me stories of 'Benny' Goodman, 'Artie' Shaw, Frank Sinatra and all of the greats of the forties. I listened to his stories and let him reminisce. That is the joy. Watching his face as he reminisces. I can never hear those stories enough because he lights up when he speaks and is so passionate about his music."*

- **A favorite restaurant.** *"Eating at Norms! Really? Such appreciation for egg whites, sourdough toast, fruit and cottage cheese!!! 'DYNAMITE!'"*

Geri's journey with each parent, while very different, are both challenging. She draws on her own personal strength and her love of family to not become buried in sadness, but rather to continue to create happy memories. She connects at the most personal level – through sustained eye contact, through music, through favorite foods, through touch, and through selfless service to her parents. She creates joy moments. She will remember them always. Geri chooses joy.

A Story about Quiet Joy

Joy is not always exuberant. It is not always a "jump up and down" experience. Sometimes joy is a quiet feeling, held deeply within your heart. For Alyce, who has been an almost full-time caregiver for her mother for four years, this quiet joy comes from *"knowing that I am able to help her and make her life more comfortable."* Alyce chose the role of caregiver. She is dedicated. She is extraordinarily gentle and kind. She has learned to find joy.

A combination of difficult events and circumstances dictated that Alyce bring her mother from a small town in Central Minnesota to live with her and her family in Southern California. May, who is now 97 years old, had been living alone in her own home. She suffered a series of falls, and although May didn't break anything, she became weaker and struggled to walk. She needed assistance with bathing, dressing, getting to the bathroom and, ultimately, was confined to a wheelchair. When attempts to secure services that would maintain her mother's independence in her own home were unsuccessful, Alyce had brought her out to California a few times, hoping that would be the solution. However, her mother always missed Minnesota and returned back every time.

Alyce tried several different options as she attempted to meet her mother's needs. Of course, geography was a big disadvantage. Limited finances were also a disadvantage, precluding full-time in-home care or a quality assisted living community. The answer seemed to emerge when a niece and her three children, who lived in May's local area, needed a place to live and agreed to provide care in exchange for lodgings. Unfortunately, the niece was not up to the responsibility, and good care was not forthcoming. May wanted to stay in her home so badly that she never complained.

The situation was further complicated by a serious infection that set in to May's prosthetic elbow. After trips to the Mayo Clinic, a few stays in skilled nursing care, and the refusal of the assisted living community to allow May to move in due to uncertain continence issues, Alyce finally brought her mother to California to stay with her — permanently.

I asked Alyce if she had some "joy" stories to share about caring for her mother. At first, she said that "joy" wasn't the first thing that came to mind, but she would think about it. I later learned during Alyce's interview that her mother had been very critical of her while she was growing up. Even to this present day, she will pick at Alyce's clothes and hair, which Alyce said, "*Still annoys me some.*" Also, her husband *"is not happy with the current situation. He thinks he doesn't get along with her – in the past, they always got on each other's nerves."* And to further possibly rob her of joy, Alyce naturally feels tied down. It's hard to take a vacation. Her brother, who lives in Atlanta, has come to stay so that Alyce can get away. *"Even just going out to lunch with friends, I have to make sure she is safe. And it is hard on me physically, mainly my back. I go to yoga three times a week to help my back."*

So where does the joy come from? Alyce, after giving it much thought, realized that joy *is* a part of this caregiving experience, not only for her but for her mother as well. First, there's the satisfaction that Alyce feels from making her mother's life more comfortable. She shares, *"I don't know where she would be if I weren't able to do this."* Alyce also enjoys watching her mother interact with Alyce's kids (May's grandchildren), the great-grandchildren, and the dog. Alyce delightfully shares that May *"adores her great-grandchildren. They help her by pushing her wheelchair and bringing her something to drink. My granddaughter, who is less than two years old, will help fold down the bed for her great-grandma's nap."* Alyce shares that her mother will talk endlessly about *"how the great-grandchildren are always willing to help out." Simple joy.*

Alyce has now been able to find pleasure in her mother's company. She takes her to church most Sundays, to doctor's appointments and out to lunch. She takes May to a beauty shop where most of the customers are older. *"I enjoy watching all of the old people. I have learned that I get along well with older people; I am comfortable around them."* And mostly, May is now no longer critical of Alyce. She expresses appreciation to Alyce every night for her care. *Reciprocal joy.*

Acceptance has become solid ground for the growth of a better relationship between Alyce and her mother. Alyce has been able to move beyond the resentments of past criticisms. May has become *"more accepting of where she is now, not fighting it so much. It was hard for her to accept that she had to give up her house. She is more patient. That wasn't one of her virtues. She is more accepting of my husband – now she says nice things about him. They get along even though they think they don't." Unexpected joy.*

It is difficult to keep a positive spirit when faced with daily caregiving responsibilities. Alyce has many friends in her community who are also dealing with aging parents issues, and they offer advice and support. One friend is currently undergoing chemotherapy for an advanced stage of cancer; still, she has been eager to help Alyce by telling her stories about caring for her own mother. Alyce has extended family that come to visit, which, of course, pleases her mother very much. And Alyce says, *"My faith helps me. It is important to me. I am in people's prayers." Spiritual joy.*

When I was finished with the interview, I went outside to meet Alyce's mother. May was outside in the California sun, trimming flowerbeds from her wheelchair. When I complimented May for her efforts, she said, "You always have to keep busy." That was her motto in life. And even now, with her physical limitations, she keeps busy. Alyce has set it up so that her mother can garden from the wheelchair. May also reads from a Kindle with enlarged font, and she keeps in touch with family on her computer with email and Facebook.

When asked to describe her life now, Alyce first says, "Difficult." There is no question that it is difficult to be the primary family caregiver for an aging parent. But then she talks about what she has learned. *"I am pretty good at caregiving. And I enjoy being around old people."* Alyce's commitment to *"being kind of stuck at home"* and taking care of her mother has resulted in her living a *"less busy life, which has actually been kind of good for me. I always thought I had to be doing something. Now I enjoy reading, the computer, gardening, and I have time to see my grandchildren a few times a week with one-on-one time with each grandchild. I am content with a quieter life."* Again, this may not be resounding joy; rather, it is a peaceful joy, a quiet joy.

Surprising Sources of Joy

There's a negative and sometimes off-putting image that commonly emerges in our minds about care and advancing age. That is of the nursing home, with its line-up of wheelchairs and suspicious odors. Let me say here that some nursing homes do fit this image, but many provide excellent and loving care. For some families, the nursing home *does* become the answer to providing for a parent's full-time needs. This is not because they are "dumping" their parent, but because the need is, in fact, a 24-hour proposition. Terrible? No, not always . . . and mostly not.

Remember Patsy, whose mother developed an active life of her own, including a real estate career, after her husband died? Patsy states, *"Yet another joy was that when my mother was in the nursing home, the staff respected the fact that she was always a woman who dressed well and wanted to look nice. We always took nice, attractive clothes and jewelry to her. The staff seemed to really enjoy dressing her up and making her look nice. Dressing well was a dignity thing for her, so even if she was feeling bad, it was good for her to be all dressed up."*

I conducted a study back in the late seventies on what happens to parent/child relationships when a parent enters an institutional setting (Falde Smith, Kristen and V. Bengtson, *The Gerontologist,* 1979*).* Contrary to the professional and popular thought at the time (which is probably why the article was published), our interviews, in many cases, revealed a "renewed closeness" and "strengthening of family ties." The staff of the nursing home was able to provide care for the 24/7 physical needs of the parent, freeing the adult children to spend time strengthening emotional, social and spiritual bonds. Comments from participants in the study included:

- *"The last two years, I was closer to my dad than ever before . . . the important point is to stay in touch and let the relationship grow."*

- *"I feel more comfortable in our relationship now because my daughter doesn't have to constantly worry about me."*

- *"My son has become everything to me. He is always with me."*

Expressions of closeness; expressions of an *inner joy.*

Another negative stereotype is that of "role reversal," a concept that is often misunderstood to mean that the children become the parents and the parents the children. But listen to Kathi, who understands role reversal and cites it as a source of joy. *"Even though they (my parents) are both doing fairly well, I begin to see little hints of the role reversal. It is kind of fun. They do depend upon me more, asking my opinions on things. I take food to Mom three times a week so that she doesn't have to cook. I am enjoying the role reversal. Right now, it is relatively easy. It may get harder, but at this point, I enjoy it."* In her experience of "role reversal," she is certainly not treating her parents as children, but rather is providing parent-like assistance in a way that subtly alters the roles with dignity and respect. Role reversal is a misnomer – it is not about treating your parents like children, merely a gentle shift in how you help each other.

An Honorable Job

While reading through the newspaper on a Sunday morning, I was thrilled to discover that a famous and highly accomplished person for whom I have great admiration shares similar values on this issue of aging parents—so much so, in fact, that I immediately thought, "This is a wonderful example for my chapter on joy."

Meryl Streep is one of the great female actors of our time. An article by James Kaplan in *The Los Angeles Times* (Parade Magazine, May 2006) about this revered actor mentioned her relationship with her parents, with whom she was very close. After her mother's death in 2001, she spent the next three years as an integral part of the constant care that her widowed father required. As the oldest child in her family, she gladly took on the main responsibility for parent care. *"There are a lot of bad things about being the oldest, but that's one of the good things about it,"* she says. *"It's your job."*

In 1973, I decided on gerontology as a profession, and this was a time when many people didn't know what "gerontology" even meant. My dad would often lovingly tell me how happy he was that I was in that field. This way, I would know how to take care of him in his old age. I was actually looking forward to that! What an honor it would be! I wasn't the oldest like Meryl Streep, but I knew about aging, and *that was going to be my job! And I would be glad to do it!*

Because my dad had spent his entire career as pastor and bishop of the Lutheran Church—often having to leave my mom alone for extended periods of time— my vision was that my parents would gently age over many years. After all, they certainly deserved to experience those "golden years" together, reaping the rewards of lives dedicated to God and in service to others. I would dream of bringing over the grandchildren and watching that relationship grow. We would have conversations about life over coffee, and sometimes wine. I would help them in whatever way was necessary until they died peacefully at a very old age.

That was not to be. At the relatively young age of 70, my dad was diagnosed with an aggressive form of prostate cancer. It had already spread into his bones. I was involved in meetings with the oncologist, and I tried, as much as possible with three small children at home, to be an emotional support to my dad and my mom. However, the dying process unfolded so rapidly that I would say that I got cheated out of taking care of my dad "in his old age" as he had wanted, and as I had wanted. The time was way too short.

Even in this agony of losing my dad, I found sources of joy that came directly from him. One afternoon, he was struggling to tell me about some of the financial issues he wanted me to understand. His speech had been severely affected by radiation treatments to the base of his neck. I knew he was tying up loose ends and I began to sob uncontrollably. He smiled at me and with difficulty said, *"Kris, it is only by the grace of God that we live each day. I have had a wonderful life."* I knew his words were true, but my sadness, at that moment, only deepened.

And yet, our parents can give us joy, even when they are dying. I was holding my dad's hand when he took his final breath. At that moment, I felt only a devastating feeling of sadness and loss. Much later, I realized that even though I did not have the privilege of providing care for my dad over many years, I did have the honor of providing the ultimate loving care to my father at that final moment. Today, the sadness remains, but I can hang on to joy, knowing that I was there for him at the end.

Closing Thoughts on Joy

The stories and anecdotes in this chapter are testaments to the fact that there can be joy in providing care to aging parents, and that there are reasons to be grateful to have this opportunity. This can be a time of life to strengthen family ties and love our parents unconditionally as we "pay them back" for all they have done for us. It can be a time of healing of broken relationships, a time to learn to appreciate our parents' individuality and strengths, a time to live in the moment, a time to create joy.

In a blog for the Alzheimer's Association called "Can Caregiving Make You Happy?" (accessed February 15, 2013), Sherri Snelling, CEO and founder of the Caregiving Club, concludes, based on research on creating the "happy factor," that "many of the activities associated with caregiving are actually the principles that experts say will make us happier in our lives." Some of the principles that she mentions are clearly reflected in the sentiments of our Cast — be kind, do something nice for someone, strengthen and deepen personal relationships, practice forgiveness, be hopeful. So it may happen that you won't have to dig deep to find joy. It may come to you, naturally, as you provide care to your parent.

And as we provide this care, we also become aware of another fact – that we, the adult children, are getting older, too. Our positive attitude and loving response to our parents will set an example to our children and other loved ones, who may be providing some care to us one day.

Peter voices a closing thought about joy: *"We, my wife and I, took the ownership of my mom's care and ran the last leg of the race. We were handed the baton and had to finish strong. We wanted to treat my mother like a queen. Throughout all of this, our motto was* **'Do it right and finish well.'** *It was a joy for me to be with her when she took her last breath, and [to] kind of usher her into Heaven."*

Key Learning Points

- Within the complex experience of providing care to aging parents, there are multiple ways to create and experience joy.

- Joy can be exuberant, quiet or surprising. It may be a natural reaction or you may have to dig deep.

- Joy is a choice; that choice can be transformed into the knowledge that caring for aging parents is an opportunity and an honorable job.

Time for Writing & Reflection

1. Develop a written plan of action for incorporating a spirit of joy into your interactions with your parents, whether they are currently still healthy or requiring some amount of assistance from you. Write about how this joy will sustain you in tougher times.

2. If you don't have the time or the inclination to write a long plan, carry a small notepad with you and jot down ideas

when they come to you. Visits with your parents or phone conversations with them will likely spark many ideas.

3. Identify key interests and activities that can be turned into "joy moments" with your parents. For example, with my mom, we used music to create joy moments. For my dad, it was sports. Write down as many as you can. For further inspiration, review Geri's ideas in the section "Stories of Creating 'Joy Moments'" above.

2

...And Accept Sorrow

*"There is a wistfulness that time is
passing and my parents can't still do things."*
~Kathi

*Y*ou may be right in the midst of this complex experience of parent care. So you already know that joy is not the only emotion we feel as we strive to meet needs and lift the quality of life for our parents. If your journey of parent care is only just beginning, let me assure you that joy will definitely not be the only emotion you will experience. In fact, sometimes joy is completely overtaken by feelings of sorrow.

In gentle terms, sorrow accompanies joy as we walk alongside our aging parents – hand in hand, one a part of the other. If you are currently a caregiver for your parent(s), you might have been thinking as you read the previous chapter, that it is ridiculous, or just plain wrong, to say that there is joy; there is only sorrow to be found in parent care. I had a colleague tell me that the years she spent caring for her aging parents were the most hideous years of her life; she found only sorrow and bitterness. She argued with me about the theme of joy; she believed it was false.

My colleague has a point. There is much to say about sorrow. And because there is so much to say, this may not be an easy chapter to read. But if you listen to our Cast, and think through and feel through the many sources of sorrow, you will be empowered to capture and embrace joy and sorrow together in your aging parent journey.

The Sorrow of Loss

The sorrow of loss or expected loss can undermine finding joy in our aging experience. It is not only the loss of our parents, but as we age and find ourselves in mid-life, we may start losing our friends, our peers, our life long companions and confidantes. We *are* at that age. We may lose beloved pets, with their limited life span, that have kept us good company as our children left home. In the course of the last few months, I lost a dear friend to pancreatic cancer, had two other friends diagnosed with later stages of cancer, and had to make the decision to put my little doggie to sleep. He was my buddy and shadow for 12 ½ years. This has been a time of indescribable sadness for me.

For most of us in mid-life, though, the pressing losses are those associated with our parents. It may be their loss of physical abilities, the loss of cognitive capacity, and ultimately the loss of life.

Even though our Cast experienced so many reasons for joy, loss was tugging at their hearts and sometimes overtaking their feelings of joy. *Listen,* and know that if you are feeling sorrow, *you are not alone.*

Mike: *"There is the sorrow of knowing you're losing them and regrets about past behavior."*

Dawn: *"Parents unconditionally love you and there is so much sadness in losing them."*

Ellis: *"The sorrow is knowing that they are becoming more frail and dependent. It is difficult to see (my parent's) inability to perform certain physical tasks such as walking vigorously, running, not having the same kind of balance. I notice that my mom has some shaking. It is a sorrow to be in a different role as I see their diminishing abilities."*

Patsy: *"Seeing someone who is so vibrant, smart, witty – seeing those abilities decline is hard to watch. (It is a sorrow) seeing the light go out of somebody's eyes."*

Terry: *"My mother is physically unable to go to my son's graduation. This is a loss for my family and for my parents as a couple. This is the first time that they're not going somewhere together."*

All different types of loss; all understandable reasons for sorrow.

We so often think of hands-on caregiving as the role of the daughter, assuming that sons primarily help with finances or other practical, objective matters. Mike, the *"horrible"* son who *"discovered beer at 15 and girls at 16,"* reveals how he took on the role of caregiver with great compassion and sensitivity. He talks at length with deep feeling about the sorrows involved in caregiving, especially about the losses that his dad faced.

"With my dad, he went from such a high platform in life – he was a successful heart surgeon and a pioneer in heart surgery – to being a heavily crippled individual. He was robbed of so many things in the last third of his life – golf, travel, dancing, the ability to physically do things with his grand-children. He had multiple sclerosis for thirty years. As a doctor, he knew his disease and started managing his life to maximize his physical abilities for as long as he could. He refused to get in a wheelchair because he knew he would never get out. Probably only one in a million could live as long as he did with nine bypasses and thirty years of MS."

Loss can be sudden and dramatic, or it can be a process over time. It requires us to find the balance that will allow us to mourn the losses within a context of joy and gratitude – not an easy thing to do – often taking a conscious and rigorous effort. Mike was able to reveal such joyful pride and gratitude related to his father even as he shared tremendous sorrow.

The Sorrow of a Fragmented Health Care System

Adult children often find the health care system to be frag-mented and inadequate. Mike explains his experiences with his mother. *"We had the frustration and sorrow of her physical care in the hospital which was not adequate. The health care system has changed so much with the regulations and financial limitations. The doctors don't have the same opportunity to give true patient care."*

This can be tremendously discouraging, especially at a time of great need.

As Peter and his family faced multiple issues with his mother, they found the health care system to be impersonal, incompetent, and frightening. They even referred to one nursing home as the "*crazy place.*" They were given a range of different and confusing information on wound care, on what level of nursing care was needed, and on his mother's capacity for involvement in decision-making. They felt extremely frustrated and helpless, not knowing what the next step should be.

Terry emphasizes that the cost of healthcare can become a sorrow. "*There is concern about one person needing long term care, and then would the other one have anything left to live on due to the cost of care?*"

The difficulties of our current system of health care will persist for the foreseeable future and often are out of our control. However, in chapter 4, "Overcoming the Obstacles," we will talk more about the health care system and how, at the very least, we can better equip ourselves to work within the system and obtain more effective and compassionate outcomes.

The Sorrow of Personal Pain

The sorrow that adult children feel as they care for aging parents can also take the form of an intensely personal pain. Patsy experienced the personal sorrow of not being able to fix what was wrong with her mother.

"*There is the sorrow that you can't make it better – no amount of money, no amount of care giving can make it better. I couldn't fix it. I felt like I was failing as a kid. My parents always fixed things for me and I couldn't fix this – I couldn't make my mom better. One sorrowful memory was one time after I hadn't seen her for a long time, I walked in and she came after me with her walker, pushing at me with it with anger in her movements. It was devastating to be greeted like that after not seeing her for so long."* Patsy could fix the problems of a major metropolitan city, but she could not fix her mother.

Additionally, personal sorrow and pain associated with lost opportunities may arise. *"When you take care of your sick, dying parents, you think about certain things,"* remembers Mike. *"When I was having trouble in school, Dad came to school and took me to lunch and said that I had the ability to be a doctor. He said that he could get me into medical school if I could get the grades. I was always very impressed with my dad, what he could do, but I wasn't a student. I always felt that I let my dad down. I was his hope for having one of his children become a doctor – that is part of my regret."*

Similarly, Peter's personal sorrow is rooted in regret. He expresses his sorrow as *"the regrets that I had of not knowing she was dying until it was kind of too late. The sorrow is that my mom was physically and emotionally abusive her whole life. Always there was something wrong. She was always complaining, nothing was right and I had to remove myself from her. The regret is that I didn't have the time to mend it. The sorrow was my fantasy of her being the mom she could have been and never was."*

Unlike Kathi, who found joy in her shifting role to a decision-maker with her parents (discussed in Chapter 1), Dawn felt a personal sorrow with the shift in her role with her parents. *"It used* to be," she says, *"that when you have a problem, you go to your parents. Then, in their older years, they become one of your problems."*

Personal pain can run very deep and bring up past memories and current feelings that interfere with our ability to compassionately provide care. I'm sure that you can add your own story here. Regrets, feelings of inadequacy, maybe a bit of resentment surrounding shifting roles, and other sources of personal pain are issues that need to be addressed. Sharing with others who are experiencing this same struggle can help effectively lessen our personal pain and strengthen our essential role as caregivers. You may also find it helpful to journal about your feelings of personal pain.

The Sorrow of Changing Personalities

Dawn strongly felt sorrow from her parents' changing personalities after they developed dementia. *"Both of my parents had dementia, and the staff at the nursing home never knew their true personalities, their wonderful characteristics and the beautiful people they once were."*

These feelings of sorrow about dementia deeply affected me as my mother journeyed through the stages of Alzheimer's disease. I specifically remember one of the family conferences that I had with staff members when my mom was in skilled nursing. The Activities Director was so happy that day because my mom *"was back to herself"* since she was willing to go to an activity after several days of refusing to participate. I remember sadly thinking to myself (and also feeling angry that this Activities Director could seem so happy), *"They (the staff) have no idea what 'herself' really is. They do not know her true person at all."* 'Herself' for the staff was a woman in a wheelchair, head down, but, on a "good" day, willing to attend activities. 'Herself' to me was a vibrant woman; a lovely, kind, caring and dedicated wife, mother and grandmother. I knew she would never be "herself" again.

Sometimes it was hard – and still is - to remember my mother before the days of Alzheimer's. The disease lasted for so many years and her personality became the opposite of who she had been. So when my siblings and I gather at the cemetery to remember our parents, we share the many wonderful memories of our life with mom. And those awful dementia memories begin to fade. The sorrow lessens.

The Sorrow of Geographic Distance

Geographic distance presents a situation that can fill us with sorrow and also a good deal of anxiety. Distance keeps us from knowing exactly how our parents are doing and can limit the ability to understand their needs. We often need to depend on others to assure the well being of our parents.

Terry feels the personal sorrow of geographic distance. *"I would like to be able to do more, to be more involved,"* he says. *"It is very hard to see your parents in a situation where you know they need your help and you cannot always be there for them."*

After years of being the primary caregiver for her mother, Patsy gave up that role to her sister. Her mother was in need of skilled nursing care, and the family decided that the best environment was in a small nursing home in the state of Washington where two of her siblings were living. Patsy lives in Southern California. So she, too, experienced the sorrow of geographic distance.

"My older sister readily stepped up to the role of daily visitor/supporter/laundress/go-to person for the final two years of my mother's life. I still managed my mom's accounts and property, and every three months flew the 1200 miles to visit her (even when she could no longer communicate and seemed to barely recognize me) ... part of my own way of processing such life changes and keeping a personal connection (not just being her "bookkeeper") to the very end, I guess!"

Today's technology has stepped in to help us with bridging distances. And even if we are somewhat "technologically challenged," (as my son likes to refer to me) tools such as email, texting, Skype, FaceTime and a wide variety of in-home technology support systems have become more user-friendly with each new advance. So although technology cannot replace human interaction, it can give us better information and alleviate some of our anxiety about parents living far away.

Shared Sorrows

Adult children often share sorrows with their parents as they face the challenges of these last years, months, days and moments, such as dealing with the reality of economics. Terry explains, *"Economics has a significant impact on quality of life. Economics causes worry – for example, my mother doesn't want to have her teeth fixed because she thinks that they can't afford it."* It caused Terry great pain to see his mom not enhance her quality of life because she mistakenly believed they could not afford it – nor did they want their children to pay for it. Simple problems without simple answers.

There can be also be shared sorrow over family situations. *"Another sorrow is that relatives don't come through,"* says Patsy. *"Siblings pull away – both Mom's and mine. Some relatives couldn't deal with her situation – they couldn't face the decline."* We expect that family and close friends will be able to be involved with care and understanding and provide unconditional support. That is the ideal. Often, it is not the reality. It isn't that these family members and close friends are bad people. They just don't possess the capacity to deal with the sad changes that come with the aging and decline of their loved ones. Then it becomes our responsibility, the mid-life caregivers, to provide them, the family and friends, with empathy, patience and understanding. That's not easy. Hopefully, though, with good communication and compassion, they will come through in the end.

There is shared personal sorrow. *"When the time came, he (my father) knew it was the end,"* Mike remembers. *"He told me, 'I won't be here tomorrow' and he wasn't. I said to him, 'I'll see you tomorrow,' but I didn't. He was so worried about my mother. I spent those last days reassuring him that I would take care of Mother."*

The Sorrow of Lost Religion

Religion is often a great source of comfort in times of loss and sorrow. Those who share a religious faith will pray together and support each other in difficult times, bringing an acceptance and sense of peace to the person facing decline and death and to loved ones. Religion also brings the promise of an afterlife and the hope of meeting again in another realm. This, too, brings peace.

My dad found strength in his religious beliefs as he was dying and was able to be grateful for the *"wonderful life"* that he had. His final prayer was, *"Now I lay me down to sleep . . . if I should die before I wake, I pray the Lord my soul to take."* In the course of my years of work in long-term care, the religious faith of many of the residents who were dying allowed me to be at peace with their death.

However, in Patsy's experience with her mother, religion became a source of sorrow. *"Mom was a very devout Catholic, but as her disease progressed, she rejected religion and that was very sad to see. She didn't want the priest. She flat out rejected her religion and didn't get any comfort from it. She wasn't even civil to the priest. This was a great sorrow for us."*

Mike also shares that his mother did not receive comfort from her religion at the end. When a nun came in to pray with her, she refused. *"She felt that they [her husband and herself] should not have had to suffer."* His mother was angry and possibly felt abandoned by God. It was a sorrow for her family that she could not feel the comfort of the promise of religion.

Religion is a promise, a hope, but it is not a certainty. For those who find comfort in the promise, that is a source of joy. If our aging parents find peace through their religious beliefs, we can be grateful. But if those religious beliefs and traditions fall short and cause sorrow in the last chapter of life, we need to recognize that too. That is all the more reason to embrace our parents, in the here and now, so that they do not feel alone.

The Sorrow of Lost Time

Finally, our *Voices of Experience*, our Cast, talked about a simple sorrow, a sort of melancholy that they, and I'm sure many of you, feel as we reflect upon our aging parents and upon our own aging. That is the simple sorrow of time passing, of not being able to go back in time and be young again, of not being able to bring back the years and maybe slightly alter the outcome.

Kathi shares, **"There is a wistfulness that time is passing and my parents can't still do things**. *There is a part of my dad that would still love to be involved in the business. With my mom, she would probably like to hit tennis balls again."* If only we could turn back time – if only.

Coping with the Sorrows – Closing Thoughts

As I write about these sorrows, I question why our parents (and likely someday ourselves) have to end their days with so much difficulty when they have led such worthy lives. I not only question, but I long to know! As of now, I am still not close to an answer. There are few of us who are so lucky to go to bed one night feeling healthy and happy, and then die peacefully in our sleep. There is often pain. There is often worry. There is often loss of memory. There can be conflict. There can be such tremendous sadness. Still, I found a piece of the answer in the following quote by Oriah Mountain Dreamer from her book, *The Invitation*. She says, *"But if we are open to sorrow as well as joy, we can expand our ability to hold ourselves and the world in our own hearts."*

Yes, with all of this sorrow, I somehow am able to return to the theme of joy. When adult children take on the challenge of providing care to parents with the belief that it bestows an honor and an opportunity, these sorrows can be shared and they can be lessened. Shared sorrow can become a form of bittersweet joy and comfort as you share at the most intimate personal level. Knowing that, through whatever sorrow that has been thrown in your path, you are helping your aging parents to live a fuller life – even if that only means that they are not alone. *Someone cares. Someone loves. Joy.*

As Peter spoke to me of his mother, he shared a story that brings him both sorrow and joy – a beautiful example of how joy and sorrow are intertwined. *"I had one really perfect moment with my mother. When I picked her up on that day, I said to myself, 'I'm going to be like Jesus and give and love.' I went to see her with a servant's heart. It was a warm, Indian summer day. We drove down to Laguna, sat together by the beach. I wanted to do whatever I could do to make her comfortable and happy. There was real satisfaction because I took a different approach to her."*

Eyes welled with tears, Peter continues, *"Because of that day, that perfect moment, I was able to write my mom a love letter that I got to read to her a few days before she died. I was able to focus on what she gave me and I was able to forgive her. Through that process, as I read the love letter and expressed my care and love, she took a Kleenex and wiped my eyes and told me not to cry. In our weakness and infirmities, we are made strong. God was able to take over and make me strong. The love letter was a great tool – I was able to open her eyes. I was able to open that door and tell her why she was the way she was, and why I am the way I am. I was able to hear her truly say that she loved me with meaning. By taking care of my mother and father, I learned to understand myself."*

It will not be easy to embrace joy and sorrow together, one a part of the other. And sometimes sorrow will overwhelm any feelings of joy. However, if you acknowledge the sorrow, seek to learn from it, and share your sorrow with others, including your parents, feelings of joy will emerge that make the tough journey a softer one.

Key Learning Points:

- Joy and sorrow are two sides of the same coin; they go hand in hand and belong to each other.

- It takes a conscious, intentional effort to focus on the joy and the gratitude of caring for aging parents in the midst of our sorrow.

- There are multiple reasons for sorrow that can only be embraced and accepted if we remember that caring for our aging parents is an honorable job, one for which to be grateful.

Time for Writing and Reflection

1. Write about your reaction to the following idea expressed in the introduction to this chapter: "There is only sorrow to be found in parent care." How does it make you feel? What memories does it stir? How does it compare with our Cast?

2. List the sorrows that you have experienced with your aging parents or another loved one. Next to each sorrow, write down how you can lessen that sorrow with elements of joy.

3. *"But if we are open to sorrow as well as joy, we can expand our ability to hold ourselves and the world in our own hearts."* Discuss this quote with your parents, your siblings, your children and/or your friends. What does this mean to you? To them? Will you internalize the message of this quote? How?

3

"Helps" for Providing Care

— ❤ —

"My wife took care of me so that
I could take care of my mom."
~Peter

H elp! I am so busy with work, with kids' demands, with countless er-rands, with house projects, with keeping fit, with my finances, with important email, with _____, with _____, with_____! I have to run over to my parents' house to bring food, help with housework, and review their fi-nances. Help! This is more than I can do! How am I going to meet my par-ents' needs and my own needs at the same time?? This is too much! Help!!

This plea for help may be your plea. The words may not be your exact words, but the feeling may be the same. You are over-whelmed with the demands of your own life, and now you find yourself at a time when you need to incorporate helping your par-ents into your schedule. This is not only physically overwhelm-ing, but emotionally challenging as well. Where can you turn to for help?

Our mid-life voices, our Cast, speak in agreement on the most important resource for the answer to the plea for help – *other people!* You are not alone, and it is imperative that you ask for help from the other folks in your life.

They are many and varied. You may not have even thought of some of the people that you can ask for help. Or you may feel hesitant to ask for help. But give it a try. You will be amazed at the response.

Other People May Be Your Parents

First and most importantly, you can turn to your parents for help – yes, *your parents.* Before you jump in to help and start to tell them what you think they need, talk to your mother and father about how they perceive their needs, what their expectations are, and who they know who could provide information and assistance.

They may have friends who are having similar concerns who have tapped effective resources. They may have had experiences with their own parents and have very specific ideas about what they want and *do not* want in terms of help from their adult children. Remember, they have already lived quite a long life, have coped with the ups and downs (including raising you), and have most likely acquired a perspective and wisdom about life that will help to navigate the sensitive road to finding the balance of maintaining independence and receiving help at the same time. They have, over many years, built their own foundation of knowledge and relationships that they can draw from and share as you figure out together the best course of care to take.

Other People May Be Your Spouse or Significant Other

In varying degrees, your closest partner may provide practical assistance, an understanding of caregiving concerns, and/or maybe a shoulder to cry on. It is imperative to ask your partner for what you need and accept the level of help that is realistic for your specific relationship. Clear communication about what your needs and expectations are will keep the guesswork out of how your partner responds in a helping role. Let that person know if you want advice, hands-on assistance, or just somebody to vent to about the frustrations of caregiving.

Mike tells us, *"What helped me most was having a very understanding wife. Also, with her availability, having parents to care for and young adults still in the house was not an issue."*

Having a spouse who has been through this experience can help to ease the tension that can surface when one spouse is devoting a great deal of time to an aging parent. Patsy says, *"My husband was great and he had been through the same thing before."* Patsy's husband was even willing to provide hands-on help when her mother was struggling. *"My husband patiently showed her week after week how to operate the heating and air thermostat, her hearing aids, and the TV remote and he posted little drawings with basic instructions for her."* Based on his previous experience with his parents, he knew what to do, and he knew how to help.

Peter answers without hesitation when asked what helped him most in coping with providing care to his mother — his wife. *"Big time – in every possible way. She made me face the challenge. She was my cheerleader, my psychiatrist, my pastor, my doctor, and she showed me how to love my mom. She challenged me to get past things.* **My wife took care of me so that I could take care of my mom.**"

A particularly poignant example of how Peter's wife supported him in difficult times took place when his mother's skin had become especially dry and they bought a deep moisturizing cream for her. Peter assumed that his wife would take over and apply this cream, but she told him no, that he was going to put the cream on her hands. Peter, who we have learned had never been close to his mother, says, *"I didn't want to touch her, but this allowed me to get closer and closer to my mom. I can still feel my mother's hands, her touch, feel her little bony hands and give her my love."*

Other People May Be Your Siblings

When we think about siblings, the first thing that probably comes to mind is sibling rivalry. However, siblings can be a tremendous resource when planning the best strategy for assisting a parent. This will be especially true if you take the time, even before your parents actually need assistance, to discuss the multi-faceted care issues with your siblings, and blend them into the foundation of support that you are building to ease the parent-care journey. Communication and resolution about sibling misunderstandings will also strengthen this foundation.

Ellis says that *"having a really close confidante to share this experience with – my sister in particular"* is what helps her in providing care for her parents. As Ellis and her sister share the joys and sorrows of this time in their parents' lives, they have also gained a new understanding of each other.

My siblings and I developed a "division of labor" to help in the care of my mother based on our own individual strengths. My mother had Alzheimer's disease, a particularly devastating disease. We split up the responsibilities of visiting, involvement in medical care, and financial planning. Our ability to share what often seemed like an enormous burden was an essential way for us to cope with our own feelings and have energy left to help her and love her. I will share in more detail about how siblings can work together when I tell you my mother's story and other stories about Alzheimer's disease in chapter 6.

Sibling support is not an option for some. Our Cast member, Dawn, was an only child and bore the whole weight of the worry for her parents. So if you are fortunate and have siblings, strategize with them to help your parents and to help each other.

Other People May Be Friends (of Yours or Your Parents)

Turning to your friends can be a good solution for finding objective input, helpful feedback and even hands-on assistance. Your friends can often fill in the gap if family is not able to give the help that you need. Patsy affirms that she found additional help from *"the support and resources of close friends."*

Dawn, the only child, also found help from *"receiving comfort from good friends – they were sympathetic listeners."* It is often true that the best help that you can give or receive is supportive listening.

There will be times when there are simply no clear answers, or no acceptable answers at all to finding an approach or a solution to a parent's needs. That's when you really need a friend to talk to and hold on to tightly. I serve as that friend, because of my experience in aging issues, for many of my friends who are searching for answers. I've become sort of the "go to" friend for aging parent problems. Sometimes I can answer their questions. Sometimes I can direct them to helpful resources. Sometimes I can ask them the right questions so that they discover some new options that might work. Other times, I can only listen.

Your parents likely have friends, too. These may be friends that have known them and loved them for a lifetime. Friends with a long history to draw upon. Some of these friends may have already discovered effective resources to deal with aging concerns and will want to help in whatever way possible.

Terry, whose parents live across the country, shares that, "*It also helps a great deal that my parents have a network of friends – through church, a caring neighbor, and the man that my dad works for* (his dad is in his late eighties). *This network allows them to maintain their independence. Their neighbor, who I check in with when I visit, is able to tell me how my mom is doing.*" Terry does not hesitate to call on this network of friends for information, for help, for reassurance. They do not hesitate to help him.

Other People May Even Be Your Children

Sometimes we don't involve our children when our parents start to decline – we think maybe it will be too hard, too depressing, too uncomfortable. But maybe we sell our children short with this train of thought and should reconsider their capacity to accept the changes that come with aging and their ability to love unconditionally. Helping grandparents can be a wonderful opportunity for them. Listen to what Ellis shares.

"It is a great help to see how my children can take up the slack," Ellis says. *"I feel really proud of them and it gives me some relief. My children don't feel that it is a burden to help their grandparents."*

I want to pause here and share the many and important ways that Ellis' two daughters were an integral part of their grandparent's care, especially with their "Mamam" as she started to decline. They displayed an extraordinary capacity to be not only deeply caring, but were also beautifully creative in their approach to helping their grandparents.

First, there was what Ellis calls "the typical things," driving their grandma to the doctor or dentist and assisting her during the visit. They would go to Starbucks and buy their Mamam's favorite, a white chocolate mocha latte – she had developed quite a sweet tooth late in life!

What's more, these two daughters went way beyond running errands and providing transportation. They would assist Ellis in distracting their Mamam so that she would be more receptive to bathing. They would turn on a little heater to warm up the bathroom and play her favorite music – Perry Como singing "Papa Loves Mambo, and Mambo loves Papa." Their Mamam would then sing this song at the top of her lungs as these two loving granddaughters gently took her hands and led her into the bathroom. She had forgotten her protests; Ellis and her sister could then take over and give their mom a shower *"in the bathroom that was so hot you sweltered but it was filled with love."*

As Ellis' mom, Anne, became less mobile, her dad, Frank, their "Pop," made his wife breakfast in bed every morning. That sweet tooth was present even in the morning, so oftentimes he would serve her pie, which she loved, and was one thing that she would eat. She also loved ice cream in the morning, and would go through a type of ritual, saying, *"Let's have something good to eat."* Ellis and her girls would yell, *"Ice cream!"* and if Pop had forgotten to buy the ice cream, her girls would go out of their way to go and buy some so that their Mamam had something good to eat – yes, ice cream for breakfast.

When Ellis was tied up at work, her girls would go over to their grandparents' house to walk their Mamam around the block.

When their Mamam began to have issues with incontinence, they were even willing to help with that – not an easy thing to do. Anne had finally agreed to wear a type of Depends that looked like panties. But when they were wet, she would throw them off and hide them in the corner behind the door of the bathroom. Ellis had moved out-of-state by this time so she couldn't monitor this situation. Her oldest daughter, Cara, lived with her grandparents, and she would check every day to make sure that her Mamam hadn't thrown the panties in the corner. And she would make sure that her Mamam was clean and smelled good.

These young women, Ellis' daughters, Anne's granddaughters, brought joy and laughter into their Mamam's life. They would drive her around, going fast around the corners so that Anne would trill, *"Rrrrrrrr"* and everyone in the car would laugh. Ellis says, *"I think the thing I loved most was just the sheer laughter my children brought into her life."*

It was the small things; it was the big things. It was buying a Starbucks; it was help with incontinence. Ellis' daughters were *other people* that she could turn to for help.

Other People May Be Others with Similar Experiences

You might be surprised that help comes from people that you don't know very well but who are in a similar situation. There are support groups for almost every type of difficulty in life. Caring for aging parents is a huge issue and support groups abound! They can be found in community centers, senior centers, adult day care facilities and churches, just to name a few. Or, you can go online and find a group that is right for you. You might be hesitant at first, but I want to assure you that in reaching out to others who understand, your thoughts and feelings will become part of the foundation of support that you are building. That foundation always needs new layers.

"It helps to talk to others who are in the same situation," says Terry, *"and share the pros and cons and all that you have to deal with."*

Dawn tells us *"that it helped to connect with people that were going through the same thing. Looking back, I wish I would have taken the time to find a support group that was a good fit for me."*

Patsy poignantly sums up the value of this category of *other people.* She reveals that, *"A great help was talking to other people going through the same thing, talking about the ugly parts of it, talking to people who can help you forgive yourself for not always doing the right thing, for not being able to fix it."*

And There's Help through Research and Resources

Knowledge is the other great help for providing care to aging parents. If you are in any way reluctant to spend the time to gather knowledge, remember that in gaining comprehensive knowledge about all things aging, you are also ultimately helping yourself. Knowledge will help you to navigate the health care system and the many aging services that are in the community. It will also mitigate the worry and fear that may be keeping you up at night.

Sometimes, an adult child is fortunate to have essential knowledge through his/her work. For Dawn, her profession in long-term health care was the source of her knowledge. *"Being in the aging field, I had knowledge of resources and options – I had a whole menu of options. I also knew that not all nursing homes were bad. When I had my parents in a nursing home, I made sure that the staff knew my parents as people. I talked to staff about their histories. I hung pictures of when they were young, as they were before, so it didn't seem like they had just always been old, demented people."* She knew the importance of something as simple as hanging those pictures because she had been in the rooms of countless older people in nursing homes, some with pictures, some without.

Patsy explains that, *"it helped having a background in social services, even though it was hard to apply my knowledge to my own situation. You do know, though, that there are answers, and so it is easier to stay calm and have some faith in the system."* As Patsy previously shared when talking about the joys of providing care, she "likes to learn," and so she took on the challenge of gaining the knowledge that she needed related to care issues.

With knowledge as a tool, she found "wonderful care places and wonderful caring people" when her mother needed 24-hour care. *"When the time came for my mother to transition to a skilled nursing facility, my husband, niece and I traveled together with my mom and moved her into a wonderful facility in a tiny town in the Pacific Northwest that is home to two of my siblings and many more relatives . . . we settled her in and I stayed awhile to ease the transition."* Patsy's social work background gave her the confidence to move forward with a difficult change and the sensitivity to support her mother throughout the move.

Most people don't have a professional background to draw from when finding resources and making care decisions. But everyone can learn! And now, so much information is readily available online. I can't stress enough the absolute necessity to educate yourself now about community resources, home care, adult day care, senior housing, levels of care within residential or nursing settings, medical conditions, medical and adaptive equipment, in-home technology resources — even if your parents are healthy and active. This knowledge will be a tremendous help to you and to your parents, and you will avoid that dreaded emergency situation in which no one knows what to do.

If you are not at all prepared as needs emerge, you and your parents will find yourself in a steep learning curve and your decisions may not be based on adequate information. Involve your parents as much as possible and as much as they are willing to participate in this information gathering. Know your options, know your community, learn about insurance, become acquainted with each parent's physician, talk to professionals in the aging field, and *talk to your parents*. Then when you have that "defining moment" when you realize that you may need to provide some amount of assistance or care to your parents, you will be well prepared.

One More "Help"

Some people also have an additional help. It's a belief in God or a higher power to whom they turn for strength and wisdom in their changing role in relation to their parents. Not all of us have this belief, but for those who do, it is a great source of power to take each step in caring for our parents.

This is true for Kathi. When asked what helps her most in her new role as a caregiver for her parents, she thoughtfully shares, *"Maybe it is my faith in God. I feel like this is what I am supposed to do. I feel called to fill this niche. My sister has her family – I have the flexibility of being a single person – it is really a gift that I am single. This is something that God would want me to do. It really comes out of thankfulness. I have been so blessed, that this is an obvious result of that gratitude."*

Yes, Many Options – Closing Thoughts

So if you are asking, "Where can I turn for help?" turn to other people, including your parents, and ask for help. They will give it to you. If you have a reluctant spouse or sibling, turn to your friends. They may not have answers, but they can lend that all-important listening ear. Turn to your children – they have a great capacity for love and acceptance. Reach out to people in similar situations even if you do not know them well. And if you believe in a higher power, pray!

And turn to yourself! Take on the challenge of learning as much as your brain will hold about the available resources that will support you as you provide care to your parents and help them to remain as independent as possible. As you will see in the Epilogue of this book, resources are abundant! You are not alone.

Key Learning Points

- You are not alone in your parent-care journey.

- The most important resource for finding help and support in providing care for your parents is a wide variety of other people, including family, friends, support groups, and for some, a higher power.

- In addition to reaching out to other people, it is imperative to educate yourself about the many resources for housing, healthcare, and social services for older people that are available in your community.

Time for Writing and Reflection

1. Sit down with your parents and ask them how they perceive their current and/or future needs. Write down their responses. Then write about how you might help to meet those needs and share your ideas with them.

2. Brainstorm with yourself, your siblings and your friends and write down all of the possibilities for "other people" who you may be able to reach out to for help and support with aging parent concerns.

3. Begin to develop a written resource list of agencies, organizations, associations, senior communities and other community resources. Make notes about each one and familiarize yourself with their services and how to access them.

4

Overcoming the Obstacles

"The biggest obstacle was my parents' resistance
to make changes in their lives."
~Mike

"Do you know how hard it is to communicate with you?
"Do you know how hard it is to try to
hear what you are saying?"
~An exchange between Ellis and her very hard of hearing father

As we have discovered, other people are the greatest resource for finding help and support as we strive and struggle to assist our aging parents to live with quality and dignity. We look to our aging parents, partners, siblings, friends, our parents' friends, even our children, and sometimes to God. Other people are the key to survival. However, other people can also become the biggest obstacle to finding solutions, even when the solutions seem clear. These "other people" obstacles are usually those who are closest to us. So *listen to* our Cast so that you can learn and hopefully avoid, or at least minimize, some of the obstacle pitfalls.

The Obstacle of Our Own Parents

These "other people" who often hurl obstacles into the difficult, winding pathway of providing parent care are the parents themselves. Yes, this is true! So say our Cast when asked about the obstacles to caregiving. The number one answer was "my parent(s)." As Mike says, ***"The biggest obstacle was my parents' resistance to make changes in their lives."***

This was a source of hair-pulling frustration at times, but also gave adult children a clearer and more insightful view into the minds and hearts of their own parents. As older people try to cope with the changes and losses that are occurring in their lives, sometimes long-held beliefs and attitudes come to the surface – beliefs and attitudes that children were not aware of, or had never taken the time to understand.

In these older years, when parents may feel that they are losing so much, it may seem like one more loss when adult children step in to try to help. Parents can become an obstacle to providing the very care that they need. Frustrating, but completely understandable!

In the gerontology field, we often say, as a *huge* generalization, that people don't change as they get older, they become even more of what they have always been. Personality characteristics and attitudes that have worked well over the years may now become obstacles. Independence may become stubbornness. Frugality may preclude obtaining necessary resources. Strength can turn into denial. Strong leadership skills may become an overly controlling nature and an unwillingness to cooperate. Pride may interfere with good and wise decisions.

Reluctance to Spend Money

An attitude that surfaces frequently in today's generation of older people - it will very likely change as we baby boomers move into our seventies and beyond - is a strong resistance to spending money to enhance their living environment or hire services that may be beneficial. Older people of today, in their eighties and nineties, have memories of the Great Depression and continue to value thrift and saving money. It is also often true that older people hold on to their assets because they aren't sure how long they will live and they want to leave money to their children.

Mike found this type of attitude particularly challenging since his parents were very well off. As he says, *"They had millions of dollars in the bank, but lived as though my dad were a box boy."* Mike understood their experience of living through the Depression, but he found it discouraging to not be able to convince them to make certain changes. He wanted them to move across the street from him, but they didn't think they could afford it. He wanted to make changes to their home so that it would better suit their physical needs, such as wider hallways since his dad was in a wheelchair. They said they couldn't afford that either. In the end, Mike says, *"We had to respect their decisions about these things."*

That is not easy to do, stepping aside and respecting a parent's decision when it clearly seems like the wrong decision. But respecting a parent's decision, as hard as that might be, is essential to maintaining a healthy relationship and essential for upholding personal dignity. Keeping the relationship strong may serve you well when some really tough decisions come up that concern safety and critical health concerns. It's sort of like putting money away in the bank for a rainy day. It is building the relationship foundation. You will have shown your parents that you are not just trying to take over. You have strengthened your relationship, and may be able to draw on that for future, complex decisions.

But, do you really want to know the truth? The truth is that if you force your decisions upon your parents, they will not accept them internally. They will not thrive even if they agree to what it is that you want.

Resistance to Using Community Resources

Another common attitude creating an obstacle to care is a resistance to researching and actually utilizing community resources that might be available and helpful. Again, this generation of older people often has less experience contacting outside resources and are therefore more likely to be uncomfortable having other people come into their home. Asking for and receiving help has not been their life experience. Helping professionals could be considered strangers and seen as an intrusion into their private space.

Terry tells us that, *"My parents are resistive to checking out resources. When I suggest they call someone for assistance, they say, 'we don't know how to do that.'"* Even for something that seems so natural for adult children, having someone come and clean the house, Terry's parents would always have a reason not to follow through. Any intervention on Terry's part, especially because he lives at a distance from his parents, needed to be indirect and very gently and thoughtfully presented. Sometimes that worked; sometimes it didn't. He believed that the bottom line was that his parents really did not want to ask for outside help, not that they didn't know how.

Kathi's mother, Marian, knows that having a full-time caregiver in the home for her husband is the only solution for them, but coming to terms with that wasn't easy. Following throat surgery to remove cysts on his vocal chords, her father has required a surgically placed feeding tube because he cannot swallow. He also needs some assistance with activities of daily living that Kathi's mother doesn't possess the strength to provide.

Yet, for her mother, having someone else in the house for 14 hours a day is "making her crazy." She has lived in her home for decades, doing things a certain way, having her things in certain places. The caregiver "puts things in different places and does things differently." Even though she feels grateful to have a steady caregiver that her husband likes and can depend on, she breathes a sigh of relief when he goes home for the night. She is a great example of someone who has been able to overcome her discomfort of having a caregiver in the home because she was able to stick with it long enough. It took constant encouragement from her daughters to realize the important benefits of in-home care for her husband and for herself.

If a parent does resist in-home help, sometimes you can propose, *"Just give it a try. It doesn't have to be permanent – just give it a try."* Or you can suggest that the extra help is for you, not for them. *You* need a break!

For some older people, they simply won't allow someone else to come into their house. For over 20 years, my sister's mother-in-law lived by herself. Since she could not see well, she absolutely refused to let anyone come in to clean her home, do her laundry, or make repairs. Part of that was fear of others due to her limited vision. Strangers in the home might somehow take advantage of her. The other difficult barrier stemmed from her insistence and unrealistic belief that she could take care of herself. Eventually as her health deteriorated, she did allow a visiting nurse to come in to take care of her swollen legs and my sister was able to convince her to sign up for Meals on Wheels. Sadly, though, when she died at the age of 94, her house reflected the rather sad condition of her life – it was not well taken care of. That had been her choice – a tough choice for her family, but her choice.

Issues of Pride, Control and Abusive Personalities

When strong personality characteristics interface with the aging process, obstacles to care may abound! These situations will take a deep level of understanding and a tremendous amount of patience.

Pride is a problem for Ellis' strong, Dutch father. Ellis shares that her father's pride gets in the way of his relationships and also causes him to overreact to other people's actions. *"As an example, in certain situations, dad is kind of paranoid and thinks that no one wants to take care of him, like he is a non-person. His doctor cancelled an appointment and now he feels that the doctor doesn't want to be bothered. This is his pride speaking."* Now her dad doesn't want to see that doctor anymore even though he has received good care from him. He lets his pride overcome his reason, creating barriers to care.

Let's return now to Kathi, whose father had been a highly successful car dealer. He started out as a car salesman, and when he retired, he owned multiple dealerships. His need to control, a strong personality characteristic, presented a bit of an obstacle in the search for a physical therapist. Kathi shares, *"He went through nine therapists before he found someone he wanted."* Her take on this was that this was more about her father than the therapists. The good news here is that he did have choices, that the family and medical professionals remained patient, and that he eventually found a therapist that he was comfortable with. Obviously, though, her father's therapy was delayed significantly as he searched for the perfect therapist – at least, perfect for him.

And for Peter, "My mom herself" was his biggest obstacle – the essence of who she had been throughout her life. She had been difficult and sometimes emotionally abusive. He didn't have memories of a once kind and loving mother to pull him through the tough times toward the end of her life. Rather, he had to dig deep within himself to find the strength to really be a loving son and stay by her side. He had to draw from a foundation that his wife had helped him to build in only recent years; a foundation cemented by the importance of family, accepting limitations, and providing love and unconditional support.

The Challenges of Dementia

When a parent has dementia, this may be the most difficult obstacle of all. With dementia, you lose the ability to anticipate a parent's reaction. You may encounter a grateful heart one day, then an angry, hostile response on a different day, or even on the same day or within the same hour or minute. In this circumstance, you as the adult child must have the courage to persevere with patience no matter what the reaction, and the strength to love in the most difficult of circumstances.

One of my closest friends, Geri, who you met in the Joy chapter, finds herself currently immersed in the emotional rollercoaster of helping to provide care to her mother who has Alzheimer's disease. One day, after a particularly distressing day of mixed emotions and unpredictable responses, Geri approached her mom as the professional caregiver was getting her ready for bed. Geri shares:

"I know Mom feels peace when she hears Ave Maria, so I put it on. She was lying down and she even sang a few words and of course had her arms and hands going as she conducted. Then she said 'Stay here with me' and I said, 'Of course. I'll lay down next to you.' I lay down and put my arm around her body and held her. She said she loved the music. I just held her. Then I put my head on her shoulder and was now in 'child' position instead of 'mom' as I have been to her for the last two years. I cherished it. We were holding each other. No words.

We were feeling each other's presence. We were. It was different. It was a clear reminder that, although we have caregivers, WE the children are her soul. She feels us. She needs us. She has been shaky and scared and she was not tonight. We lay together and listened to two more Ave Marias and then I saw her eyes were closed and she was at peace, so I carefully snuck off the bed, like I used to do with my children. Ahhh, peace..."

Providing care to a parent with dementia requires us not only to be knowledgeable about care options and resources, but also requires us to delve into the depths of our being to overcome the huge obstacle of providing care to a parent who may not know who we are; who may hate us for what we are trying to do – only because they no longer understand. Geri took a risk. Her mother had been nervous and shaky and would sometimes react to touch with anger, even violent behavior. But Geri drew on her instincts, knowing that her mother loved the music of Ave Maria. The result could have been very different; her mother *could* have become angry and pushed Geri away. But that night, Geri's love and courage allowed for the peaceful ending of the day.

We'll take an in-depth look at the many facets of caring for a parent with Alzheimer's in chapter 6. Even within the parameters of this heartbreaking disease, there are ways to cope and reasons to have hope.

The Obstacle of Family Dynamics

Family dynamics can be another daunting obstacle in exploring options and making decisions with aging parents. Old, worn-out family roles and behaviors can come into play and block the path to understanding and agreement. There might be feelings about who is the family favorite, who Mom and Dad listen to best (regardless of actual knowledge of the situation), or who carries the greatest burden of family expectations.

Perceptions of Parents Toward Adult Children

Ellis describes her family dynamic with some amount of frustration. Although she is the gerontologist with years and years of experience, her father considers her sister, who is a successful businesswoman, to be the source of reason and decision-making. *"My dad will hear and act on the news if it comes from my sister."*

Her father considers Ellis to be the emotional one and doesn't always recognize that she is actually the expert! Ellis recognizes that *"It is important that I don't see this as a slight – different children have different abilities and a parent will choose who to listen to accordingly. On the other hand, for me, my dad relies on me for warmth and compassion and on my children, his grandchildren, for joy."* Not a bad trade-off! And Ellis' sister does understand that Ellis is an expert and will get advice from her before offering possible solutions. They have had a good partnership.

Perceptions of Siblings Toward Each Other

Siblings will often have differences of opinion and different levels of understanding of their parents' situation. Terry, who has the complication of living at a great distance from his parents, expresses this well.

"I have three sisters and there are three different levels of communication. One of my sisters, who is local to my parents, is still very dependent on them and she isn't really able to help. The sister who lives close to me has not had any experience with elderly people and she also has the distance issue. She has a hard time accepting role reversal and is constantly amazed at what my parents can no longer do and the simple things that need to be done to help them. She sees it as much more complicated, when, in fact, just some daily life tasks need to be done – activities of daily living. She has a hard time accepting the state of affairs – and that much of what our parents need is just basic. I have a hard time understanding her lack of understanding."

Terry also has an additional family dynamic obstacle that I have heard about countless times over the years from adult children as they talk about their parents. Oftentimes, the parent's expectations of their adult children can be unrealistic. For Terry, he says, *"my dad thinks that my sisters who live close to them should be able to do everything that mom did, but my sisters can't clean and cook all of the time."*

A cry for help often comes from adult children who are trying to do more for their parents than they can actually manage. Remember the importance of building a stronger foundation of relationship with your parents as you start to tackle some of the smaller problems that emerge? When your parents expect too much, this is a time to draw on the strength of that relationship and have an honest conversation about what you can do and what you cannot do. The emphasis, of course, should be on what you can do, and then come prepared to offer alternatives for those tasks that you really cannot do. Honesty is the key, here. It will be counterproductive if you tell them that you can do it all, but then you can't follow through.

Perceptions of Adult Children Toward the Aging Parent

Sometimes the differences of opinion among siblings can preclude care altogether. My dear friend Joann, who lives in Delaware, had been trying to coordinate care for her mother, who lived alone in Florida. She has two sisters who are both nurses and lived nearby to mom.

Joann visited her mother regularly and found that she was not taking care of herself. Her mother was not bathing, not cleaning the house, and becoming more and more of a pack rat. Meals on Wheels was delivering food but her mother was stacking all of the food in the refrigerator until it became spoiled. So of course, she was not eating well. Increasingly she was becoming more confused. Joann's sisters continued to insist that Mom was doing fine and could take care of herself. Joann could only surmise that her sisters were in denial. Or perhaps are very good nurses to their patients at work, but not to someone with whom they are emotionally involved.

After several months, the situation deteriorated to the point that Joann decided to just take charge. She has now brought her mother to live with her and is very creatively working out ways to make this situation successful. Her husband, in the meantime, is spending much more time in the garage pursuing his hobby of making furniture – she says she will have plenty of chairs!

Joann is one of those determined persons who took on the challenge of networking throughout her community and educating herself about the available resources in her area. She makes those resources work for her situation. Her mother is in adult day care three times a week. She utilizes respite care so that she and her husband can go on vacation. And they have made her mother's room cozy and comfortable with a Lazy Boy recliner and an electric fireplace, purchased from the Amish community. The décor includes a mantle that looks like a mini-fireplace and actually throws off heat. This is gradually keeping her mother in her own room in the evening when Joann and her husband would like to be alone.

Joann says, *"I honestly don't care what my electric bill goes to if it buys me some time alone."* I have told Joann numerous times that she would win a "Daughter of the Year" award for the commitment that she has to assuring her mother's well-being throughout these difficult years.

The Obstacle of Our Own Denial

We, the adult children, can be big obstacles to working with our parents on care solutions, as Joann's sisters were, without even being aware of it. This is often because we are in denial that our parents have chronic problems that may mean that life is coming to a close for them – maybe not imminently, but the clock is not going to turn back. And unless we are dealing with an acute, curable condition, things are not going to get better.

What does that mean for us? It means that we are getting older, too, and the balance in life has shifted. Hence, the denial. The current cliché that 60 is the new 40, may be somewhat true due to healthier lifestyles and advanced technologies. And there is a huge positive to that mind set. Yet the truth is that if our parents need care or, as in my case, we have lost our parents, we are facing situations that will not allow us to deny our age. We are the key to decision-making for our aging parents and we are at the top of the family line. We, very simply, are on the aging journey – no room for denial.

External Obstacles

There are also external obstacles that impede our quest for working with our parents toward the best quality of life. A clearly obvious one is our fractured healthcare system. In their interviews, members of our Cast expressed, as a source of sorrow, that the system was impersonal at best, incompetent at worst.

Healthcare is a critical area in which you must equip yourself with knowledge and be prepared to be an advocate for your parents. Patsy says, *"You have to be a sophisticated consumer to deal with the whole age-related industry . . . as a family, we had to learn about all of these things – bill-paying, insurance, Medicare, HMOs."*

There is a complex system of hospitals, long term care facilities, assisted living homes, in-home health care and/or homemaker services, community resources such as senior centers and adult day care, adaptive durable medical equipment for the home, information and referral agencies, aging life care professionals, and in-home supportive technologies. The list is long and continues to grow.

It is our job, as adult children, to be educated about the resources that are available, know how to use them, and work with our parents to understand their meaning within the context of their needs. And today, with online resources, there is no limit to what we can learn! We can blame the health care system for not being good enough to provide what our parents need, or we can work with it through knowledge and courage, and optimize what it has to offer.

Kathi learned the importance of being an advocate for her father in the hospital setting. Following his surgery, the social workers behaved rudely to her mother, first insisting that he be placed in what Kathi and her mother considered to be a substandard rehab facility, and then pushing for him to return home before he was ready. Kathi says, "There was a real push", but she and her mother knew that he was nowhere near ready to return home. They decided not to be intimidated by the social workers and not blindly follow their recommendation. They went directly to her father's physician, who interceded on their behalf. Her dad remained in the appropriate care level until the necessary arrangements could be made for optimal care at home.

Technology can turn on older people and become an obstacle. Research tells us over and over that older people effectively continue to learn and adapt, but at a slower pace. Yet, technology races on. Everything becomes faster by the day – computers, tablets, smartphones, digital everything, long menus of choices to get simple information. Combined with the speed of how technology changes, many older people have sensory deficits in vision and/or hearing which can make it very difficult to process important information. Sometimes it might take a lot of patience to work with your parents and help them really get the information that they need.

It is within this context that we hear the interchange between Ellis, who is trying to explain health information on the computer, and her dad, who is very hard of hearing. In frustration, Ellis exclaims, ***"Do you know how hard it is to communicate with you?"*** to which he replies, ***"Do you know how hard it is to try to hear what you are saying?"***

It is probably true that if you find yourself to be frustrated and impatient with your parents over something they are unable to do or understand, they are likely far more frustrated than you and probably feel quite vulnerable as well. Take a deep breath, and muster all of the patience that you can – it is essential! Put yourself in their shoes! They may be trying to catch the world, perhaps with limited sight, hearing, and mobility, only to have it speed by, and leave them wondering what it was that they were supposed to do.

A Myriad of Obstacles – Closing Thoughts

So I say to you – yes – the obstacles are many. And your parents may be the biggest obstacle of all. But please believe me when I tell you – and I know because I have been through the heartache of terminal prostate cancer with my father, and Alzheimer's disease with my mother – you can overcome the obstacles and help to fill the essential, significant pages in the final chapter of your parents' lives.

Have honest conversations with your parents. Throw away old family roles, habits, and expectations. Don't let the health care system intimidate you but rather transform yourself into an advocate. Face that denial about your own aging so that you can help your parents deal with their losses and sadness. Take a deep breath as you seek to explain the complexities of their situation.

And remember to walk in their shoes. Think about what it would be like to not see well, hear well, or understand well. Think about their fears as they approach the end of their lives. In the end, if you can do nothing else, hold them and hug them – because touch is the sense that never fades.

Key Learning Points

- Our own parents, due to long-standing attitudes and personality characteristics, may be the biggest obstacle to securing the help and services they need to enhance their quality of life. An awareness of this dynamic and respect for our parents' views are critical for problem solving and relationship building.

- Family dynamics as well as our own fears about aging can also create barriers to effective care planning and implementation.

- The obstacles and complexities found within our health-care system are especially challenging and require adult children to be educated advocates for aging parents.

Time for Writing and Reflection

1. Write down one or two personality characteristics of one or both of your parents that you think might lead to difficulties in how they adapt to the changing circumstances that come with aging. How will you approach a situation in which a parent creates an obstacle to care and/or services? Write about the strategies that you might use.

2. Now reflect on yourself. Write down one or two of your own personality characteristics that might create an obstacle to future decisions about care and services. How would you want your adult children to respond to the obstacles that you are creating?

3. If you have not already done so, begin your research on the healthcare system and the specifics of your parents' health network. Start a file with your notes and assessments about their health conditions, their physicians and specialists, and insurance information. Continuously add to this file as you discover new aspects of their health-care issues.

5

The Healing Touch of Laughter

"At least I didn't drop the pie"

~Dawn's Father

I think I may have developed a warped sense of humor. At least, you might think so as you read this chapter. Many of my fellow colleagues in gerontology have this same warped sense of humor. In fact, if you had been a fly on the wall at some of our staff meetings when we were discussing certain residents of our long-term care community and laughing to the point of tears, you may have thought we were somewhat cruel as well. You could have interpreted that the laughter was at the expense of the very people that were in our care. The truth was, however, that we were not laughing at our residents. We were laughing about situations that while difficult and sad deep within, also contained an element of humor. And sometimes, we needed to laugh.

I remember one time in particular, when our chaplain of the Lutheran long-term care community where I worked for years, was telling us about serving communion to our residents who had significant memory loss. He would have the residents sit around a table when he would offer the bread and wine. I don't know how many of you reading this are familiar with the "bread" that is offered in the Lutheran Church (I think something similar is used for the Catholic Church and some other Protestant denominations as well) but it is a round, flat, white wafer type thing that looks and tastes nothing like bread and practically chokes you when you try to swallow it. In fact, it looks more like a poker chip or a carom game piece than bread and it tastes like cardboard. There was one resident who I'm sure at one time was likely very devout, but every time our chaplain would hand him the communion "bread," the resident would set it on the table and flick it across the surface as though he *were* playing some type of game. It actually makes me laugh as I am writing this – See? *Warped!*

Now, of course we could have focused on how sad it was that this man could no longer understand the elements of communion, and to some degree we did. But the thought of that white, flat, stick-in-your throat wafer being flicked across the table was really the making of a great opportunity to laugh! We laughed so hard, we cried! A close friend recently told me that her mother, who has advancing dementia, and whose husband still takes her up to communion, takes one look at that white, flat wafer and sticks it in her pocket! I'm fairly certain that isn't what the pastor intended!

At our long-term care community, we gave ourselves permission to have a shared deep-belly laugh about this and many other situations. This lifted our spirits and enabled us to carry a little bit lighter load. Laughing helped us work more effectively and lovingly with our older people and their families.

And sometimes, we would just share a gentle laughter to lift our spirits. One day when I was having a work-related conversation with the President and CEO of the organization that I worked for over many years, we somehow moved from our work topic to losing our parents. We had become friends as well as colleagues and were also acquainted with each other's parents, so the shift in the conversation was natural. In fact, he knew my father quite well. When you work in a long-term care setting, these death-related conversations are rather spontaneous and frequent.

In the course of this interchange, we both shared that we weren't quite sure about heaven, whether or not it is an actual physical place. Could our parents possibly be up there having coffee together, having a good time, and getting to know each other better? What a great image! As we were both raised in the Lutheran Church, the question about heaven was a serious one.

The CEO then shared that when his mother was dying, he asked her that if there was any way that she could let him know about an afterlife, to please do that! He shared that he had always been a person of hope more than a person of faith. This resonated strongly with me. I had asked my dad to do the same thing! And I, too, am in the hope category. We laughed as we discovered this common bond.

As we talked about the rather fun image of our parents in heaven, we promised each other that we would let the other one know if we "heard" from our parents. From then on, when we would see each other, even if we were just walking down the hallway, we would ask, "Have you heard from your parents yet?"

And even though the answer continued to be, "Not yet," that light-hearted but meaningful sharing brought a smile to our faces and a hint of laughter to our hearts. This reminds me that I need to call him and find out if he's heard anything.

Our Cast and Humor

Thinking about the many good laughs related to aging that I have had over the years, both in my work and in my personal life, inspired me to highlight questions about humor in the interviews that I conducted with adult children. I wanted to know if they had been able to share laughter with their parents even as caregiving became more complex. I wanted to know if laughter had transcended some difficult situations. I wanted to know if laughter had brought some healing at times when it would have been easier to despair and give up.

I feel compelled to make a disclaimer before I share some of the following stories that were told to me. That disclaimer is that you may not always "get it." In other words, you may not understand why the story evoked laughter. Some of what I share is lighthearted and the humor is obvious. Other stories are more serious, and yet laughter was like the cumin in the guacamole. It is a key ingredient for a successful outcome. My apologies to those of you who do not put cumin in your guacamole – try it, though – it makes a huge difference!

As I listened to and recorded these stories, it wasn't always a deep-belly laugh that we shared in the telling. However, it was certainly a lighter moment drawn from clear memories of much-needed humor. As you read these stories and anecdotes, think about how the potentially painful or worrisome situation was lightened by humor, by laughter.

Patsy's Humor Stories

As Patsy's mother moved into an advanced stage of dementia, the family decided that a small, home-like nursing facility would be the best care option for her. Although Patsy lives in Southern California, much of her family resides in the state of Washington. Ironically for Patsy, after many years of being her mother's primary support system, the best choice in nursing homes turned out to be in Washington.

Patsy shares these stories with a wonderful sense of humor, combined with a bit of sadness, and yet, with underlying joy.

" *I would visit my mother up in Washington – I would go up at least once a quarter because I was the one in the family handling her financial affairs. During one of my visits, the staff talked to me before I went into her room- they told me that she couldn't talk anymore, didn't know people anymore. They were gently preparing me so that I would not expect much from the visit. I was feeling hesitant, not knowing how it would really feel to have my mother not know who I am. When I walked into the room, she looked at me and said, 'Have you filed my taxes yet?'"* She remembered all right!

"*Another humorous incident happened much earlier when she couldn't drive anymore. She was dying to drive, obsessing about driving. She had driven until she was in her mid-eighties. So one day, my brother said, 'Let's go for a drive.' He had a big pick-up truck. He hoists her into the big truck, puts her in the driver's seat and lets her drive. Her feet can barely reach the accelerator. She drives along with a big grin on her face, and after about a half-block, she said, 'OK, I'm done now.' She never talked about driving again."*

And a more difficult story, but still with an element of humor.

"When she was starting to lose her ability to communicate, and she needed to say things, she would try to find some way to let her needs be known. My mom was always a very kind person and never would say or do anything that would hurt another person. On this particular day, the nurse, probably wanting to either give her some medication or fix her robe for her (which my mother did not want) leaned over her, and my mom bit the nurse on the breast. We all had to laugh at this, including the nurse, who was not hurt. It was so out of character!"

Kathi's Experience with Humor

Kathi goes to her parents' home three nights a week. She brings food to have dinner with her mother and to keep both of her parents company. Her father, since having surgery on his vocal chords, receives all of his nutrition through a surgically placed feeding tube. She shares ...

"We sit in front of the TV. Dad can't talk above a loud whisper, and Mother can't hear. My dad, after trying unsuccessfully to tell her something, will finally turn to me and whisper, 'Tell her.' I have become the interpreter. Sometimes she misinterprets what he says and I have to say, 'No Mother, he

said...' We go back and forth like this most of the evening – and we laugh, we really laugh! It's hilarious!"

Humorous Anecdotes from Ellis

Hearing impairment can lead to some pretty funny conversations. In our interview, Ellis shares some of these "miscommunications" that she has with her father. She does emphasize that her family has to be sure that they are not laughing at him, *"but he laughs at himself, so we can all laugh together."* In that spirit, she tells the following ...

"Because my dad is hard of hearing, he can misconstrue what you are saying, which can be very funny. I can say, 'You are late,' and he will say, 'What? You have to urinate?'"

"Another example is when a neighbor, Mr. Buckley, called the police because my dad had his sailboat (which he built himself) parked in front of the house. My dad kept saying, 'Mr. Buttweed, Mr. Buttweed, what kind of a neighbor is that?'"

" I also remember when I was pregnant, I told him that I used a 'kit' to find out. He thought I said 'kip' which means chicken in Dutch. He asked me if now they were using chickens instead of rabbits?"

Ellis adds that *"both my mom and dad love to laugh – there isn't a day that goes by that they don't laugh. My parents' style with each other continues to amuse us – they banter back and forth, they are both so stubborn."*

And in an additional thought on humor, Ellis reveals that her mom says, "*Oh shit*" a lot. "*One day she called me a 'shithead' on the way into church. When I called her on it, she said 'Shit is not taking the Lord's name in vain.' I had to laugh – and agree with her!*"

Mike the Master of Humor

Mike is exceptional in his capacity for humor in situations that have potential for emotional disaster, especially for him, as a caregiver. As he told these stories, it was hard to record them because I, too, was laughing!

Both of his parents were having difficulty with driving, and were behind the steering wheel less and less. As a result, the cars often sat idly in the garage. Still, driving remained potentially problematic. About his dad, Mike shares . . .

"*Driving was a concern for a long time. One day I watched my dad pull his huge Cadillac Seville into their small two-car garage (he did have hand controls in his car because of his MS, so he was able to drive for about two years longer than he would have otherwise) and I decided to take the coil wires off of the car. Three months later, my dad says, 'I think I've got a dead battery.'*"

And about his mother, he tells me . . .

"*My mother was never a good driver. One day I discovered that the entire right side of my mother's car was all shredded and opened up on the side, and she only had three hubcaps. When I talked to her about it, she said, 'Oh Michael, don't say that – there's nothing wrong with the car.'*"

Mike adds to this, "*These stories are humorous, but it is very difficult to take the keys away from your parents. The car is their independence. I recommend indirect intervention in taking away the car – remove the battery!*"

Mike tells yet another story . . .

"*We bought my father an electric cart to get around the house. He wouldn't let me do the work to widen the hallways to accommodate the cart (too expensive), so he completely tore up the walls. We would put marks on the wall as to where we thought he would crash next. He was not at all mechanical. He would turn the cart on, and it would be in reverse, so he would just crash into the wall and say 'Whoa!' Then he would move forward, crash again, and once again say, 'Whoa!' He would laugh; we would laugh.*"

And one more Mike story, a very tough one . . .

"*One evening, my wife was taking my mother out for a 'girls' night out' in order to give her a desperately needed break from caregiving for my father.*" By this time, Mike's dad was in the final stages of multiple sclerosis. He could barely walk with a walker and required assistance to go to the bathroom. "*I was going to order pizza and have dinner with my father at the house. My mother answered the door, purse in hand, a look of terror on her face, ready to leave, and told me that I would have to help inside. When I started to enter, she gently pushed me back a little so as to prevent my wife from entering. She bolted out the door, as fast as her feet would take her, and left with my wife. As she grabbed my wife's arm and walked directly to our car, I routinely said to them to have a good time.*"

"*When I entered the family room, here is my father lying on the floor almost naked with clear evidence that he didn't make it to the bathroom. Quite a mess! He was so humiliated. He hadn't hurt himself but the situation required that I spend an extensive amount of time cleaning him up and reassuring him that it was OK. While he was still on the floor, and I had finished cleaning him up as well as the carpet, he looked up at me and said, 'Can we have Canadian bacon on our pizza?'"*

Mike continues, *"As we later ate our pizza, my father said, 'Isn't this fun?' We both had a glass of wine which we both drained pretty quickly."*

Mike laughs heartily as he finishes this story, an especially poignant example of how humor was able to diffuse a situation that could have only caused humiliation and embarrassment for Mike's father and for Mike. As Mike now tells this story as an example of humor, he marvels and laughs at how his dad was able to bring the whole situation back to the pizza topping – and they were both able to laugh – and eat their dinner. Pretty amazing!!

Being Open to the Humor

This may now be where you pause and ask, "How is this funny? I don't get it." Of course, these stories are not funny in the "haha" sense. But to recognize the humor that can be found in the human condition, especially as we age, is very good therapy, for aging parents and for adult children. When I asked our Cast to share a humorous story or anecdote, only one person wasn't able to come up with several examples immediately. And in the sharing of these stories, there was laughter all over again. A healing process to be sure!

There are choices to be made as we provide care to aging parents and as we age ourselves. We can be anxious or peaceful. We can be bitter or grateful. We can be depressed or hopeful. We can cry or we can laugh. Chances are we will be and do all of the above. But I would like to challenge you and encourage you to find the humor whenever possible. Don't be afraid to laugh with your parents, your siblings and your friends! And don't worry about what others might think when you need to really, really laugh to the point of tears about even the most difficult situations.

A Final Touch of Humor

In closing, these last three anecdotes speak tenderly to this theme of humor.

Peter

"A day or two before my mother went into a coma, I was feeding her an ice cream bar. She loved chocolate! The chocolate was falling all over her face, dripping off her chin – a mess! He remembers fondly, *"Instead of being upset, she laughed as she was trying to catch the chocolate, licking her lips and fingers, and asked 'What are you doing to me, Peter?' Then we both laughed. It was one of those hopeful moments."*

Dawn

*" My father's eyesight was failing. At Thanksgiving dinner, he was carrying a pie from the kitchen and tripped over his grandchild's gate barrier. He fell flat, but saved the pie. That became an ongoing joke with him. When overcoming an obstacle, he would remark, '**At least I didn't drop the pie.**'"*

Back to Ellis

A few days before her mother Anne died, Ellis was cuddling with her in her bed. Anne roused from her sleep and asked, *"How long have I been in the hospital?"* Ellis replied that she wasn't in the hospital, she was at home. *"No wonder the service is so bad,"* Anne quipped without missing a beat!

Key Learning Points

- Humor and laughter are essential ingredients for being a more effective and loving caregiver and for dealing with the aging process as a whole.

- Even in the most difficult situations with aging parents, if an element of humor can be found and is mutually expressed through laughter, the situation may diffuse and resolve without heartache.

- Humor cannot always be easily found, but it is often a choice, a choice that will enhance the well being of your aging parents and your own well being as you provide compassionate care.

Time for Writing and Reflection

1. In your current experience with your aging parents, whether or not you need to provide care at this point, write about interactions with them that resulted in shared laughter.

How did that shared laughter feel? For your parents? For you?

2. If you are currently providing care to a parent(s), write in depth about one experience in which laughter eased the situation and allowed a more satisfying resolution. Then write in depth about a situation in which humor was not expressed and how the outcome may have altered if you had interjected humor and laughter.

3. Write about ways that you can strengthen the "humor relationship" with your parents so that you can draw on that humor in difficult times. Then call them up or visit them and practice what you write.

6

Voices of Alzheimer's Disease

"The Old Gray Mare She Ain't What She Used To Be"

~My Mom

*J*t may seem like a dramatic shift to move from a chapter on laughter and humor to a chapter on Alzheimer's disease. Yet, in a very real sense, they are deeply intertwined. For an adult child who is on the Alzheimer's journey with a parent, the challenge to find humor will be almost overwhelming, seemingly impossible. But along with small elements of joy and intermittent meaningful moments - laughter, through the tears, will be there too.

I've decided to change the format for this chapter on Alzheimer's disease. Rather than writing with themes and sub-themes, I will tell you three in-depth individual stories. The richness of these stories begs for them to be told in their entirety. I do this so that you, the reader, will more fully understand the impact of how the Alzheimer's diagnosis affects those who must learn to live with it. Each has different elements in the details. All three, in their own unique way, share the themes of joy, sorrow, laughter, gratitude, intentional strategies to cope, fears, regrets and hope. And through these stories, told in detail because of their importance, you will learn valuable lessons about what to do, and possibly what not to do, if someday you are faced with caring for a parent with Alzheimer's disease.

For this chapter, I've also changed the format of the learning points at the end. Rather than brief bullet points, I have expanded them into summary paragraphs blended with themes for writing and reflection. If any of the closing paragraphs inspire you to do some writing, please do so. It's wide open.

Before you get into the *listen to* mode of these stories, I want to share some important information about Alzheimer's disease.

The Alzheimer's Epidemic

When I went to the American Society on Aging conference a few years ago, I sat and listened to numerous speakers, went to several classes, and attended a large general session, all dealing with the topic of Alzheimer's. Alzheimer's was definitely in the spotlight! Why? According to the introduction to the general session entitled, "We Must Stop Alzheimer's by 2020," "Alzheimer's Disease has become the single greatest threat to the health of aging Americans." Startling, scary, and depressing - to say the least!! This is why I am devoting a chapter to this specific disease. It is a major theme of aging.

When I first started writing, I had originally thought that sharing one story, my mother's story, would be sufficient to cover the key Alzheimer's issues. However, as with all aspects of the human condition, there is a wide range of responses to this disease – by the person with the disease and by the caregivers. Alzheimer's will affect millions of lives, so it's important that you hear more than one voice; listen to more than one story.

Again, taking from the written introduction to the general session named above, the number of people today, who are diagnosed with Alzheimer's and related dementias, is approximately five million. Due to the massive number of baby boomers that have begun to turn 65, estimates are that by the year 2050, 13.5 million people will have Alzheimer's disease. Symptoms of dementia don't usually appear before later mid-life, but the likelihood of their appearance doubles every five years after 65 – and by the age of 85, one in two people have symptoms of dementia. And the 85 plus group is the fastest growing segment of our population!

The numbers for Alzheimer's disease keep climbing because as of today, it is 100% incurable – which also means that it is 100% fatal. Other diseases, including certain cancers, cardiovascular disease, and AIDS are experiencing a decline in the numbers of persons affected. Not Alzheimer's. We were presented with the following at this general session:

> In the mid-1980s, when our country finally made a commitment to fight AIDS, it took roughly 10 years of sustained investment (and about $10 billion) to create the antiretroviral therapies that made AIDS a manageable disease. The National Institutes of Health still spend about $3 billion a years on AIDS research, while Alzheimer's, with five times as many victims, receives a mere $469 million . . . far more attention and funding are needed to keep this disease from derailing the 21st

century. To accomplish this, we must turbo-charge and accelerate the level of advocacy, funding and scientific research. Just as President John F. Kennedy, in 1961, dedicated the United States to landing a man on the moon by the end of the decade, we must now set a goal of stopping Alzheimer's by 2020.

The reality of sheer numbers makes Alzheimer's disease a top priority for assuring the health and quality of life for older adults. Plus the sobering truth that this disease, "robs its victims of memory, judgment and dignity, leaves them unable to care for themselves and destroys their brain and their identity – often depleting their caregivers and families both emotionally and financially," (Aging in America, ASA Conference, 2011), creates an urgent need and requires a powerful response to conquer Alzheimer's disease. It will not only affect the millions of persons who have the disease, but also their family caregivers, the health care system, and the many friends and loved ones who will struggle to stay in a meaningful relationship with the person who has Alzheimer's. It will touch and directly affect many of our lives. It has already affected mine.

I wish that as a result of this conference, I could now boldly proclaim an announcement of a breakthrough cure, but sadly, I cannot. If such a life-saving cure had been discovered, you would be reading about it in bold print across the media. We do have some new research in areas of lifestyle interventions in early stages of dementia that may slow the progression of the disease, which is promising. But for now, the best that I can offer to you are stories – voices - that illustrate how well families *can* cope, plan, and strive to maintain the dignity of their loved one, even when faced with this sad and devastating disease.

So now it's time to *listen to* these three important and heartfelt stories.

Listen To Stories

1. Joan and Kristen's Story – My Story

> *"I made the conscious decision to believe and hang on to all of the good and wonderful things that I had always believed about my mom. Once again, I was able to breathe. And sometimes, I could smile and even laugh."*

> ~Kristen

This story highlights the sorrow of a changing personality, a strategic division of labor among siblings, real human regrets, and ultimate gratitude for a loving, almost perfect mother.

"The Old Gray Mare She Ain't What She Used To Be," a phrase from an old children's song, was what my mother would often say when she started to notice age-related changes. It seems, on the surface, such a silly phrase, but for reasons only known to her, it seemed to capture how she felt after she lost my dad and started to deal with some physical changes along with loneliness and depression. In her final years, as she moved through the stages of Alzheimer's disease, she would recite this phrase. Even as she entered the advanced stages of Alzheimer's and said very little, she would still say, "The Old Gray Mare..." It would make us a little sad, but also reminded us that she was our mother, reciting a phrase that she had said so many times through the years. We still had a small part of her.

In my graduate gerontology education, the positive aspects of aging were emphasized over and over - wisdom, experience, "free to be oneself," second careers, volunteering, mentoring, making a difference. This is all wonderful and hopeful, and these words ring true for many, many older people. It was also easy to believe when I was 25 years old. When the diagnosis of Alzheimer's disease enters this rather glorified portrait of the passing years, those positive words become empty, and the adult children are introduced to a dramatically different image of growing older. The benevolent image transforms into one of forgetfulness, confusion, agitation, and often times, personality changes. As this devastating disease progresses, the person forgets the present, no longer understands the meaning of the future, and finally loses the past as well. The person loses a sense of self. It becomes increasingly difficult to find any aspects of joy, humor or gratitude.

My mother – the beautiful, kind, smart, loving Joan Falde – was diagnosed with "probable Alzheimer's" in 1996. I had noticed unsettling changes in her for the few years preceding this diagnosis. I had tried to attribute these changes to depression, caused by the death of my dad. I would notice her just staring off into space when I wasn't actively engaging her in conversation. We would go clothes shopping - an activity that she loved doing with my dad - and as I was searching through the racks of clothes, I would turn around to find her just watching me, not looking at the clothes at all. I wondered then, did my dad usually pick out the clothes for her to try on? I rationalized that maybe this was just her standard pattern.

She also became overwhelmed with the mail. Mail would still come for my dad and of course, she would receive all of the standard junk mail. She would call me almost every day and say, *"Kris, I don't know what to do with all of this mail."* She couldn't discern the important mail from what could be thrown away. She started to have stacks and stacks of mail everywhere!

I didn't allow myself to recognize these early stages of dementia. No one – no matter how educated, professional, or enlightened – wants to face a diagnosis of Alzheimer's disease for a loved one. In my profession, I have worked with countless older people, once vibrant and optimistic, and watched them and held them as they declined into confusion, anger, and incapacity. I couldn't believe that this could happen in my family! After all, to my knowledge, there was no family history of dementia. My maternal grandmother died at 94 years old and had a terrific mind all of those years. Besides, my mother was a good, caring person who had given so much of herself to her husband, to her children, and to God. Certainly she deserved better than living her final years with Alzheimer's disease!

Then, one day came that defining moment that I referenced in the Introduction...

My mom and I were shopping to buy her a new dress. She had some Macy's Department Store coupons for 25% off everything in the store for that day. We shopped in Macy's for close to two hours, and weren't successful in finding anything that comfortably fit. We decided to take a lunch break and headed over to the Nordstrom café. As we were eating, my mom said to me, *"We should go over to Macy's after lunch and do some of our shopping – I brought these coupons for 25% off."* I could no longer ignore the symptoms. I lost my appetite that day. I'm not sure that I ever really got it back during the next several years. It was heart wrenching to try to keep the part of my mom alive that was kind and loving, when the reality of her actual existence evolved into confusion, frequent agitation, and sometimes even apparent hatred toward me. There were times when I absolutely could not breathe.

As I stated before, a parent diagnosed with Alzheimer's disease profoundly challenges us to find good, to find joy, to find humor, to find gratitude. But they can be found, even if they come in very small, almost unrecognizable doses.

First of all, for me to survive emotionally, it was critical not to over-analyze the behavior that my mom displayed as a result of this disease. If you are at all familiar with Alzheimer's disease, you may have heard it said that there is the "happy Alzheimer's person," and then there's the "agitated, angry Alzheimer's person." This is certainly not a scientific observation, but to some extent it seems to be true. During my many years working in long term care, I knew many residents with an Alzheimer's diagnosis that, although they did not remember their loved ones or understand their surroundings, would spend the day happily talking, singing, and didn't seem to be suffering, although no one can know the inner sufferings of another. Then there were those other "problematic" persons who were angry, frustrated, combative, and said hateful things that they would have never said when they were healthy.

During one of the workshops that I attended on Alzheimer's at the American Society on Aging conference, this discussion of the "happy versus hostile" behavior came up, with different participants having one or the other experience – sometimes both. One person shared that his mother, with Alzheimer's, became so much nicer to him than she had ever been before – not my experience at all. My mom was in the hostile category.

I asked one of the presenters, who is a geriatric psychiatrist and specializes in Alzheimer's disease, *"Is there is any research available that would help us to understand these differences? He said, "No, there's not. It is research that still needs to be done."* He then said it might involve the course that the damage travels, affecting different lobes in the brain in different individuals, but there is nothing yet to confirm this idea. He indicated that this would be very helpful research in that it would help to predict and also understand behaviors. This, in my view, would allow family members to better cope with negative personality changes. It would have helped me.

Again, my mom, throughout the course of her disease, remained mostly in this hostile, angry group. For the first several years of the disease, she was still in her own home, but could no longer make sense of her environment. As a result of this confusion, she became suspicious and actually, at times, could be terribly mean. My sister and her husband had moved in with her in order to help her maintain her independence. She would accuse my sister of being someone else - someone that my sister's husband was having an affair with – she did not recognize my sister as her daughter. And she was angry!

Other times, when my sister was at work, my mom would leave her terrible messages on her voicemail, accusing my sister of abandoning her, and telling her that she hated her. When she later lived in an assisted living setting, and then ultimately, in skilled nursing, she would say hateful things to other residents, to the staff, and to us, her children.

I still feel heartsick when I remember the day that I moved her into skilled nursing. Sadly, I was mostly on my own with little help from the staff. My mom became more and more agitated throughout the day. When I knelt down to hug her and reassure her, she gritted her teeth and said, *"I hate you!"* When I collapsed into tears, the staff finally offered more help and sent me home. I cried all the way.

I share this because it is so important to understand that this type of behavior - the angry, hostile behavior - is the disease, not the person! During this time, I had people suggest to me that perhaps my mother, my shy, loving, "always there for us" mother, had always had these hateful thoughts just beneath the surface. Now, with this disease, she was finally expressing these negative feelings. Even fellow professionals in gerontology would suggest this as an explanation for her behavior. *Was this supposed to be helpful?*

I had a chance to combat this explanation at the same workshop on Alzheimer's that I just mentioned. Maybe, after all of these years, the idea still bothered me. When I asked this same geriatric psychiatrist if my mother may have been harboring these hateful thoughts over the years, he said, "Absolutely not!!" He also said that it was cruel for other people to even suggest that. The class agreed! They were angry that friends and colleagues would offer this an explanation. I felt so vindicated!!

One day, I sat and reflected at length about my mother's life and her life with my dad. I remembered my mom and dad holding hands. I remembered them going out to dinner, to the movies, to Dodger baseball games, to the Hollywood Bowl, to church, to concerts, to Europe, to South America, to our weddings, to our children's baptisms – and I decided, NO – my mom was not a miserable person whose true feelings were now finally coming to the surface. She had a wonderful life! The words and actions that were now so negative, so hurtful, so hateful . . . those were the disease. They were not who she was, they were not her past, they had nothing to do with her. They were the symptoms of a person-robbing disease called Alzheimer's.

When I came to this realization, only then could I start to look for small moments of joy. I could start to discover some humor even when her situation was so terribly, terribly sad. *I made the conscious decision to believe and hang on to all of the good and wonderful things that I had always believed about my mom. Once again, I was able to breathe. And sometimes, I could smile and even laugh.*

I recall when she was still living in her own home and had homemakers from a reliable agency coming in to assist her with making meals, bathing, and keeping her company. She would tell us that the homemaker would just *"throw her up over her head and swing her around"* in order to get her in the shower. She was not particularly upset when she would tell us this and she would act out the scenario as though she was the homemaker. This may not seem funny at first, and of course, we did need to verify that the homemaker was gentle in her approach. Once we had the confidence that nothing close to that was happening, the visual of what my mother was describing was really funny!

My father did a lot of traveling throughout his working years. When we children were young - there are four of us - my mom mostly stayed home with us and spent many evenings and nights without him. In my conversations with her during those last few years of Alzheimer's, I would talk about my dad quite a bit (he died several years before), hoping to trigger some good memories and good conversation. During one such interchange, I mentioned that dad did have to travel so much, especially when we were young. She replied, *"Where is that Gaylerd anyway? He must be out sitting on a rock somewhere!"* My first reaction was surprise that she actually said my father's name. That didn't happen very often anymore. Then the image of my distinguished, Lutheran Bishop father just sitting out on a rock somewhere, probably twiddling his thumbs in her mind, actually did make me laugh. It was a fun story to share with my siblings.

Then there were the tender moments – few and far between – but they were there. For these tender moments, we were grateful. My mom was a very shy, reserved person. We knew that she loved us, but in all of my scouring of memories, I cannot remember her telling us, the children, that she loved us. During her years of dementia, she did say, *"I love you,"*— not often, but sometimes. That was such a wonderful change from the hostile behavior.

At times, she amazed us and would do something that we thought she was no longer capable of doing. She was still living in her own home with my sister and her husband and their old dog Sammy. By that stage in her illness, she didn't know her own phone number and could no longer microwave a cup of coffee, but she could always remember to feed the dog. Then one day, Sammy died. My mother found her, covered her with a blanket, and called my sister at work to tell her that the dog had died. My sister came home right away to discover that this was true. My mom, at that moment in time, knew exactly what to do.

My mother spent the last three and one-half years of her life in a Lutheran Home, first in assisted living, then in skilled nursing. It was very difficult to make the decision to give up the family home, but one day, we discovered that my mom really didn't know it as her home anymore. She said, *"I don't know why we moved out here into the middle of the ocean."* We laughed - it turned out to be harder on us than for her to move on from that house.

Her final two years were in skilled nursing. We filled her small room with as many personal items and pictures as possible. In hindsight, we probably did this more for ourselves than for her.

She no longer seemed to recognize familiar faces or favorite belongings. It was important to us, though, to have her wedding picture, pictures of her grandchildren, a favorite cross, a scrapbook. These things reminded us of who she really was and her many years of a happy, healthy life. It was getting harder and harder to remember the good times. It also helped the staff to see her as a person, with a history, with a family, with a smile.

Visits became painful as she withdrew from her surroundings and the life in her eyes continued to dim. Our family is very fortunate that there are four children, all of whom lived close enough to visit and who all, to this day, get along. We also all have different strengths and developed a "division of labor," so to speak. My sisters lived the closest to her so they could visit the most frequently, usually with coffee and doughnuts in hand – a favorite of my mom's. With my many years of experience in long term care, I was the "family conference" representative, asking the questions, talking to the doctor, trying to ensure that all aspects of care were appropriate and thorough. My brother, an actuary, was the obvious choice for handling her finances. This was a great set-up and helped each one of us to know that we were doing something important for her and that we were helping each other.

During the last months, the one thing she did still respond to was music. My brother, who is also quite an accomplished pianist, would come and play for the residents. She seemed to feel the familiarity of the music, and would sometimes "play the piano" in the air with her fingers. It reminded us of all of the times that she sat down and played hymns. It reminded us of when she would play Christmas Carols on Christmas Eve – wonderful memories – and gave us a brief moment of joy.

Shortly before her death, she was lying down for a nap. I was getting ready to leave and went to the sink to put some water on my face. Her eyes had lost their capacity to communicate, and she no longer called us by name. Suddenly as I turned to leave, she said our four names very slowly –*"Jonelle, Gaynelle, Kristen, Gary"* – and then she said, *"It is so hard to remember."* I ran back to her bedside to see if there was something more that she would communicate. I held her hand – but nothing. Yes, it was another special moment. A brief moment of joy, my last one. Somewhere deep within her, she still knew our names. She still knew that we were an important part of her life, people she wanted to remember.

I do have significant regrets as I think back on these years that my mother had Alzheimer's. I share them, painful as it is, so that if you are facing dementia with a parent, you will not make the same mistakes.

I did not always do my best. Although I had suspicions that something was wrong beyond normal age-related memory loss, I waited too long to pursue comprehensive testing and diagnostic procedures. As a professional in the field, I have no excuse. I can only say that I fell victim to not wanting to face that my mother may have dementia. By the time I took her in for testing, which occurred over a three-day period, the testing mainly served to cause her - and me - great anxiety. When we had the family conference with the doctor, psychologist, and social worker to review her test results which identified the she had "probable Alzheimer's," she was already at a stage in which she could not comprehend what was being said. When we left the conference, she said, *"Well, at least I don't have Alzheimer's disease."* We had waited too long. This made it almost impossible to involve her in advance care planning and prevented open conversations with her about how to manage this disease as a family.

I also regret not involving my children more in visiting her and being a part of this experience. At the time, I wanted them to remember her as she was, and not have their memories be of a grandma who didn't know who they were. In hindsight, I think I made a big mistake. Very likely, they would have been able to accept her situation far better than me. And very likely, they would have offered me much-needed support. They would have also learned important life lessons about suffering, compassion, and unconditional love.

Additionally, we were not careful enough with the home caregiver situation. Since we were working with a very reputable agency, we didn't feel the need to thoroughly check on my mom's daily activity. Plus my sister and her husband were living with my mom, although they were at work all day. When her monthly financial statements arrived, we felt comfortable setting them aside until my brother could look at them. This went on for several months. After all, my mom wasn't spending any money. But we received a terrible shock! When my brother did open all of those statements to do her taxes, he discovered that the caregiver was regularly taking her to the bank to withdraw cash, cash that the caregiver was then stealing. The agency was bonded and we pressed charges against the caregiver, recovering most of the money. And by court order, the caregiver was not able to pursue the LVN credential that she was pursuing. But for this to happen right under our noses is something that all four of us remember with shame and sorrow.

My final regret is that I was not with her when she died. I could have been, but I wasn't. Her condition had been so much the same for months and months and months. Then one day, she took a downward turn. I arrived to find her outside with my brother. She was up in a wheelchair, but would not raise her head, would not look at us. It was as though she was just closing out the world entirely. When the nurses put her in bed for a nap that afternoon, she never again got up and out of bed.

My sisters and I spent most of the following day with her. When I left, I asked the nurses to call if her vital signs began to change. I had been able to do so little for her over the past months – there was nothing I could do to ease her suffering, and she was suffering. But, I thought I could be there with her, holding her hand, when she passed from this world.

I had seen this downward turn before in my professional experience with persons who had Alzheimer's. I just assumed that she would live another week or two, so I did not stay that day. I thought I had time. I didn't. *Never assume.*

I was busy. It was the weekend, the weekend before Christmas. My daughter was performing a major role in The Nutcracker. A registry (temporary) nurse was on duty. He did not call. I was not there, nor was anyone. My mother died alone. And the truth is that I still can't fully forgive myself.

So in the midst of this sadness, emerging into a more hopeful place, let me share my heartfelt pieces of advice to you about caring for a loved one with Alzheimer's disease:

- As soon as you observe any symptoms that seem out of the realm of "normal aging," take your loved one for an assessment. Today, in 2017, an early diagnosis can lead to interventions that may slow down the progression of the disease.

- Put together a team of family and friends that can each use their different strengths to share the responsibility, the burdens, and the occasional moments of joy.

- Don't hesitate to involve your children in the interactions with your parent. They may provide the greatest joy and will learn the importance of compassion and caring in all circumstances.

- Keep your sense of humor.

- And, always remember that the difficult, and sometimes hateful behavior is the disease, not the person.

My mother died three days before Christmas in 2002. It had been a long and difficult journey. Yet, as we, her children, reflected on her life, we knew that in spite of these last years of confusion and suffering, she would say, if she could, that she had a wonderful life. The shy girl from Minnesota, who married the pastor who moved out to California and then became a bishop, experienced 45 years of a loving marriage, raised four kids, enjoyed her grandchildren and traveled the world.

It may have been true in those final years that, ***"The Old Gray Mare She Ain't What She Used To Be,"*** but that didn't make her any less our wonderful mother, our dad's devoted wife, or her gentle, gracious self. We are grateful for her life, for the many ways that she was there for us through childhood and into adulthood. We are grateful for the brief moments of humor and joy that we could glean from the last years of her life's journey.

2. Barbara and Diana's Story

"I am ready to let her go and am trying to hold on
to the happy memories of the mother she was to us . . .
It will be a huge loss and a void in my daily life
and I am trying to prepare myself for this."

~Diana

This story reveals the relief that comes with the "happy" manifestation of Alzheimer's disease, the importance of specific and forward-thinking strategies for financial planning and care planning, the joy of a new relationship within the realm of dementia, and the bittersweet acceptance of the Alzheimer's journey.

Diana is an accountant in her sixties, whose mother, Barbara, was diagnosed with Alzheimer's disease in January of 2003. Diana is married, has two sons, both in their twenties, and two sisters who live out of state. Her father Thomas, who Barbara always called Tommy, died suddenly of a heart attack in 1994. Barbara, who has now been a widow for 15 years, was 76 years old when she received the Alzheimer's diagnosis. She is currently 84 years old, and is now in the final stages of the disease. Diana is not aware of any family history of dementia.

When her mother received an Alzheimer's diagnosis in 2003, after undergoing comprehensive testing at the University of California, Irvine (UCI), Diana was not surprised. She had suspected it for a while. She had started seeing symptoms, small signs, as early as 1999, maybe even sooner. There were moments of forgetfulness, moments of confusion. Barbara asked the same question over and over. She had once been an impeccable dresser, but that had faded away. Diana no longer trusted her mother to drive out of fear for her safety.

She recalls that during that time, her sister, who lives in Colorado, needed some help because her husband was having brain surgery. Her sister only wanted Diana to come, not their mom. She could not really trust that Barbara would be able to help; it was possible she may only cause more anxiety. She particularly didn't want her mother to drive her grandchildren to their activities.

Another early symptom appeared when Diana was helping her mother to obtain long-term care insurance. The application involved a rather lengthy in-home interview, and Barbara did not do well on the memory portion of the exam. She was able to procure the insurance for three years, but not for the extended time for which Diana had hoped.

Barbara took a trip to Ireland with a friend in 2000. The friend reported that Barbara didn't handle the trip well. She couldn't handle the currency and became confused. She brought home strange, small gifts – items that she would never have purchased in the past.

Then there was a trip that all three daughters took with their mom to Catalina in 2001. During this trip they decided that Barbara's forgetfulness could no longer be attributed to normal aging or possibly depression. They decided together *"our mother needs to be tested for her memory problems. "*

At that point, Diana didn't talk to her mother about the possibility of Alzheimer's. Although Diana was close to her mother, Barbara had not openly and emotionally shared about important life issues—issues such as the death of Diana's grandmother and the serious nature of a medical procedure for her father. Diana describes her as "very closed," probably in an attempt to protect her children from life's burdens, rather typical behavior for someone of her generation.

Diana's strategy during this time was to take her mother to her primary care doctor and have the doctor administer a mental status questionnaire as part of her physical. She still didn't yet say anything to her mom about her suspicions of Alzheimer's. According to the doctor, her mother did well on the memory test, so at that point, Diana says, *"I let go of pursuing an exact diagnosis. But I did begin to intentionally and more frequently help my mom in ways that would allow her to maintain her independence. I gradually began to handle my mother's finances, always mindful of honoring her dignity."*

When the diagnosis became certain, there was concern about the care recommendations. The health professional at UCI told the family that Barbara needed full-time care. She stated that there was a danger that she might leave the stove on or do other things that could endanger her well-being. To Diana and her sisters, this recommendation seemed very premature. Their mom was in the early stages of dementia and was still able to do many things for herself. Diana decided to take her mother to the University of California Los Angeles (UCLA) for an additional consultation. As she said, *"UCLA is the best of the best,"* and she wanted to ensure that they were doing everything possible to help their mother. The doctor at UCI had prescribed Aricept, a drug that may help to slow the progress of the disease. At UCLA, the doctor also put her on Namenda, which is often prescribed for later stages of Alzheimer's and works on different areas of the brain than Aricept. Studies do indicate, however, that neither of these drugs has much impact and may only serve to slow progression of the disease in very early stages. In a lecture that I attended very recently on brain health, the presenting scientist stated that currently there are still no medications that have shown any definitive results of improvement in the brain scans of persons with dementia.

During this comprehensive assessment process, Diana chose honesty with her mother and told her that she was being assessed for the possibility of having Alzheimer's. Her mother didn't argue about it. When the diagnosis came in, she only said, *"Your father would have had a hard time with this."* She seemed to understand her diagnosis, but didn't really talk about it. She did tell her friends

- she had a close- knit group of women friends in her community - but would mispronounce the word and say that she had "Alkheimer's."

For a few months following the diagnosis, Barbara continued to live alone in mild stages of the disease. Diana and her family had pursued an early diagnosis. They didn't wait for a crisis to occur. Diana did go over almost every day to check on her. Her older son was attending college close to his grandmother's house, and he would stop by after school to check on her as well.

Barbara was able to continue with her activities. She had a large network of friends. One favorite function was a group called the 'buggy club.' It was a travel group and the women would take turns planning the trips. Although Barbara continued to participate in this group, she was no longer able to take her turn to plan.

A major concern during this time was the driving issue. Diana went to the DMV after her mother was diagnosed, but they informed her that they could not take her driver's license away based on the daughter's information about Alzheimer's. Diana was incredulous! It was time for her mother's license to be renewed but she only had to take the written test. She studied and studied – Diana even helped her to some degree even though she didn't want her mother to pass the test. Diana decided to be what she called "not 100% honest" and told her mom that the doctor said she couldn't drive anymore. Barbara seemed ready to accept that, and then after several tries, was unable to pass the written test. So the driving concern was resolved.

Then in May of 2003, Barbara called Diana and said she couldn't breathe. She was taken to the hospital and diagnosed with congestive heart failure. During her stay in the hospital, Barbara became extremely disoriented, constantly trying to pull out her IV tube, very uncharacteristically running down the hall, gown wide open, saying she was going to take the bus to go shopping. Hospitalization for persons with dementia is often traumatic. To the hospital's great credit, instead of instituting restraints, they placed a volunteer at her bedside, 24 hours a day, to help keep her calm and comforted.

Again, the family was told that she needed 24-hour-care. Although the severe disorientation subsided after she left the hospital, Diana and her sisters decided that she should have 24-hour in-home care. A major part of this decision was the fact that their mother needed to take medications four times a day – medications for the congestive heart failure and medications for Alzheimer's. In consultation with her sisters, it was reluctantly agreed that this would be more than Diana could do on a daily basis. Diana did have a husband, two boys, a career – and she needed to have some balance in her life. And with her sisters both living out of state, there was no one with whom to share the immediate responsibility. Diana did her homework, contacted the Alzheimer's Association and a well-respected Alzheimer's facility, and was referred to an agency that provided the home care that Barbara now needed.

Overall, the in-home caregivers worked out well. Over the three years that Diana's mother received this care, she had only three sets of caregivers - full-time and relief. At first, Barbara resisted having a live-in, insisting that she didn't need it. To complicate the situation, her group of friends agreed that she didn't need this care. Diana shares that her mother, left to her own devices, would dress to go shopping and be in a robe, bobby socks, and heels. But when someone was helping her dress, when she was going to an event with her friends, she was dressed well, and her friends didn't recognize the problem. There were times that Barbara would have diarrhea, and without cleaning herself, would put her clothes on over it. These are the things that happen.

The family wisely decided to take precautions before the in-home help started. As we learned in my mother's story, even the most reputable homecare agencies may unknowingly have dishonest caregivers. Diana removed her mother's valuable items that could easily be stolen and replaced them with less expensive pieces. Her mom didn't notice. Diana didn't want to leave anything portable in the house that would be a significant loss if it were taken. But again, her caregivers worked out well and theft was not an issue.

Of course, even in the best of circumstances, there are others who are waiting to criticize. Diana had set up a system to allow her mother to withdraw $20.00 a week with a debit card. Barbara liked going to the bank and Diana believed that this would give her mother a feeling of control. However, in a conversation that Barbara had with one of her friends, the friend interpreted this in her own way. She began telling others that Diana was making her mother live on $20.00 a week. Diana, understandably very upset by this misinformed accusation, finally called this friend to explain what the reality was. She says, *"The frustration of doing your very best, only to have others who really have no understanding of the situation, or are in denial of the true circumstances, jump in and criticize, adds to an already almost unbearable burden."* That Diana had the courage to call this friend and set her straight is a tribute to her own strength and to her commitment to her mother's best interests — interests which Diana had an inherent ability to understand.

Just a few months following the decision to hire 24-hour in-home care, Diana went to an attorney to check over her mother's will and trust and update those essential documents, if needed. Her mother did not have an advance health care directive, so the attorney drew one up. Fortunately, end-of-life decisions were addressed in the trust/will, so Diana knew that Barbara did not want any *"artificial prolongation of dying if continued health care would not improve her prognosis for recovery or enjoying a productive life."*

In addition, the family set up a durable power of attorney for management of property and personal affairs. All three sisters are on these documents but can act alone on their mother's behalf if needed. With the sisters living in three different states, it is paramount that in the case of an emergency, only one signature would be needed.

Diana became the sole trustee of her grandparents' and parents' trusts, which was recommended by the attorney. Since Diana is the daughter that lives in close proximity to her mother, this arrangement was agreeable to her sisters. Diana is able to manage all financial matters, sign and make changes, and quickly handle the estate upon death. She does send an accounting of all financial transactions to her sisters, something she initiated on her own. All of this works very well for this family because they are close and they trust each other. This type of detailed planning has alleviated some of the stress associated with Barbara's declining health.

Diana and her older sister did discuss the advance health care directive and all of the financial documents with their mom. But as with other difficult issues, it wasn't something that Barbara wanted to discuss at length. Diana says, *"She agreed and felt comfortable and secure in signing all the papers. At this point she understood that she was not able to handle all this and was happy that we were responsible for it."*

During these three years that Barbara was in her home with full time in-home care, she did have periodic episodes with her heart, going to the emergency room a couple of times. Her confusion was starting to be more apparent. She would call her friends up to 10 times a day. That tends to be when friends start to distance themselves. Barbara even began to distance herself from her regular activities. She also started to wander the house at night; during the day, she would often just sit and watch TV.

With Barbara's combination of heart problems and Alzheimer's disease, Diana and her sisters began to research long-term care facilities, particularly those that specialize in service to persons with dementia. Their mother was still high functioning, but they wanted to plan ahead. They wanted to know what was available. Again, they didn't want to wait for a crisis and then not have a solution.

A possible crisis loomed in their minds. Barbara's home had two stories—the staircase was steep and narrow. She had started to wander the house at night so there was deep concern that she would fall down those stairs and fracture a hip or possibly sustain an even more serious injury. Diana's house did not have an available bedroom (both boys were still at home) so having Barbara move in with Diana was not a viable consideration. Diana still tried to think of other options. Perhaps they could buy a more manageable one-story home for their mother and continue with 24-hour live-in care. It would be difficult to go through a move like this; Barbara would have to adapt to a new and uncertain environment. There was no assurance that this could be a long-term solution. And in discussion with her sisters, Diana realized that this could actually cause more burden than benefit.

On April 1st, 2006, Barbara again was admitted to the hospital for complications related to congestive heart failure. It was at this point that Diana, Susan, and Cathie, the three daughters, the three sisters, decided that, following hospitalization, their mother should be placed in the Alzheimer's facility that they had already selected as the best one to meet Barbara's needs. Diana's sisters particularly pushed for their mother to move into an Alzheimer's home. They knew that the burden on Diana was heavy since she lived closest to their mom. And although they visited often and were involved in all of the key decisions involving their mother, the day-to-day responsibility fell on Diana. With saddened hearts, all three sisters agreed that when Barbara was released from the hospital, the best decision was to have her move into the Alzheimer's care facility.

When Barbara first walked in to the Alzheimer's care facility, she said, *"Please don't do this."* She knew. The first days were very hard. Barbara grew visibly upset and repeatedly said that she wanted to go home. Diana recalls that for the first few months, her mom continued to ask to go home. Although Diana knew that the care facility offered much more stimulation and social interaction than her mother could have at home, this was a difficult time and Diana wondered if they had placed her too early, if maybe she could go home.

Then something wonderful happened! Barbara met Charles. He became her boyfriend, her constant companion. They began to do everything together. They went on outings, played bingo, and were always holding hands. Diana and her sisters totally accepted this relationship even though Barbara seemed to forget their dad. They were able to find joy in this relationship because it was the catalyst for Barbara to adapt to her new environment. This acceptance is not always the case. I have known many adult children who insist that their parent be separated from someone with whom they are developing a relationship, claiming that mom or dad would never be in the relationship if they didn't have dementia. They are "protecting" their parent from an "inappropriate relationship." However, they may also be taking away moments of happiness.

Barbara also took on the role of caregiver for other residents. She would always help her roommate. Diana feels that her mother held on to her life's philosophy of making the best of things. She put her old life aside. She made a new life and helped others when she could. Diana says, *"My mom's personality really hasn't changed. Even now, she is still very proper."*

Barbara has now entered the final stages of Alzheimer's. Physically she is still strong, but she walks only short distances with a walker, is assisted with eating since she mostly just pushes her food around on the plate, and doesn't talk much. Diana shares, *"She will say a few words, but the words come out garbled. She then stops, like she knows the words aren't right. She isn't agitated; she always seems happy. She giggles in response to questions or conversation. Sadly, she no longer participates in activities, and recently has started to fall asleep every few minutes."*

Barbara gets tears in her eyes when her family comes to visit. She still recognizes them. Her grandson, who used to visit her regularly when she was in her own home, had not been visiting his grandmother in the care facility. He said he didn't want to see her this way. Diana didn't push it. But recently, with coaxing from his girlfriend, he did visit her. And although *"he left with tears in his eyes, he was happy that he had finally gone to see her!"*

Barbara has lost Charles. He had been in the hospital. Upon his return, he was in a wheelchair, and Barbara didn't remember him, rejecting his company. But Charles was a determined suitor, and Diana also encouraged the relationship. Barbara and Charles did return to their former relationship for a time. When Charles went to the hospital a second time, she only asked for him the first day. Diana explained that she didn't know what his condition was. He didn't return to the facility. She didn't ask any more. By the time Charles died, Barbara had forgotten him.

Even with her diminished capacities, other people are still drawn to Barbara. Although she is declining into the later stages of Alzheimer's, she has something special, something unique. Now, she has a new best girlfriend.

As Diana, Susan, and Cathie observe their mom, they agree that she no longer has a quality of life. They have realized over the past few months, *"She no longer communicates much, has great difficulty walking, needs help eating and sleeps all the time. A year ago, she was going on daily walks, participating in activities, still coming to my house (Diana's) to visit and seemed to be happy."*

When asked about grief, Diana says that she is feeling an "anticipatory grief," already grieving the loss of her mother's fully capable self. Diana was hoping that they would never get to the point where they are today. Then she poignantly expresses, ***"I am ready to let her go and am trying to hold onto the happy memories of the mother she was to us. I know that when she passes it will be extremely difficult for me because I see her several times a week. It will be a huge loss and a void in my daily life and I am trying to prepare myself for this."***

As Diana thinks back over the years that her mother has had Alzheimer's, she can find reasons to have joy. She found a lot of joy in her mother's relationship with Charles. She shares, *"My mother's ability to connect with another person at this point in her life certainly added a dimension of purpose to her life."*

Diana also finds joy in the fact that she knows that she and her sisters selected the best environment for her mother. This Alzheimer's care facility has wide-open spaces where the people are brought together; no one sits isolated in their rooms unless they are sick. Barbara was always a social person, and the spacious set-up of this home was clearly the best fit. I also sensed, as Diana shared her story, a joy in the easy and comfortable collaboration with her sisters on some very difficult decisions. Susan and Cathie do not live close by – but they were always available in an emergency and were fully involved in deciding how to best provide care for their mother. The three sisters are emotionally very close.

Diana can find reasons to laugh. Although she knows that in a way she was laughing at her mother, she says she had to make light of and laugh when her mother went tearing down the hall of the hospital, open-robed, to go shopping. Diana laughed when her mother didn't want to stay long at her house or even visit at all once she had connected with Charles– *"She wanted to go back to Charles!"* And she laughed when the nurses told her of Barbara and Charles' nighttime routine. Charles would walk her to her door; then Barbara would want to walk him to his door; and they would walk each other back and forth until the nurses would gently intervene so they would say good night and each go into their own room.

And Diana has reasons to be grateful. *"I am grateful that even in these stages of dementia people are still drawn to my mother. I am particularly grateful that my mother's personality has not changed. She didn't go through the angry, hostile stage that so many persons with Alzheimer's do. Even in these later stages of the disease, she seems happy and likes to be around other people. She doesn't seem to suffer. And I believe that my mother still recognizes us; her teary eyes are a clue."*

The strategies and care solutions that Diana and her sisters researched and utilized have turned out well. Diana used to think that they may have jumped the gun in both getting her in-home care and then later placing her in a facility. Perhaps her mother could have lived on her own a bit longer; perhaps if they had installed some additional safety items in the home such as an alarm for the front door, Barbara could have stayed in her home a bit longer. Perhaps.

Now that Diana has had more time to reflect on these decisions – and it was something we discussed at length during our conversation – she has come to realize that to plan ahead, to prepare, and to make a decision before a crisis occurs is a good path to follow. She says, *"I sometimes felt that we were moving too fast and somehow accelerating the disease . . . but maybe we did help avert some possible problems and disasters by being prepared and making decisions BEFORE problems could arise."*

Of course, there are no right or wrong answers when it comes to making these important care decisions. You can only make the best decision at the time, based on the information available and the perceived best interests of the person receiving care. So Diana has mostly found peace with the decisions that she has made, with full confidence that her mother's best interest is always her main concern. The caregivers worked out well; the Alzheimer's care facility is providing good care to Barbara.

When asked what advice or recommendations she would give to someone whose parent has been diagnosed with Alzheimer's, Diana didn't have to think about it.

She quickly volunteered:

- Plan ahead.

- Look at all your options.

- Study your finances so that you know what you can afford – Alzheimer's can go on for many years.

- Be prepared and keep your parent safe.

- Keep your parent in the home as long as you can.

- Know your resources – looking online helped a lot. I also called the Alzheimer's Association, talked to many friends, and got referrals.

- When dealing with tough decisions, such as driving, you don't have to be 100% honest with your parent. I decided it would work better if I told my mother that the doctor said she couldn't drive. But when it comes to the diagnosis of Alzheimer's, then you have to be completely honest. You have to tell them.

When thinking about her own life and her own aging, her mother's Alzheimer's diagnosis is terrifying. Diana hopes that scientists will come up with a cure, or that they will discover medications that have a greater benefit than those that are currently being prescribed. Diana is starting to take more vitamins and supplements. Even though she is in excellent shape and exercises regularly, she is exercising even more. She intends to keep working, read as much as she can, intentionally exercising her brain. She shares that her mother never worked outside of the home; she didn't read much or engage in activities that would exercise her brain. Her main interest was in social activities. Diana is trying to *"keep my mind really active."*

She says that it is the initial diagnosis that is so frightening. But then as Diana reflects upon her mother's life, she recognizes that, *"My mom had a great life."* And even now, Diana feels that her mother *"has a better life than other older people who may have clear minds, but are suffering with illnesses that cause great pain such as cancer or severe arthritis. My mom doesn't seem to suffer. And I take great comfort in that."*

Knowing that her mother's life could have been much worse - that she is not in pain as are many others, and until recently has had a good quality of life - has helped Diana walk this Alzheimer's journey with her mother. But she also knows that she doesn't want her children to walk this same journey with her. Just as she so expertly planned ahead with her mother's financial and personal affairs, she is doing the same for her own life.

As we finished our conversation, Diana was somewhat apologetic, saying that perhaps I wouldn't be able to use her story to speak to and teach others because hers was a "cushy" case. That is, they had the financial resources to pay for in-home care and to place her mother in the Alzheimer's home of their choice.

I said this to her and I say this to you – there is no "cushy" case of Alzheimer's. Yes, Diana's family is fortunate that the financial component was not a source of concern. And if your family has financial limitations, you may have to look harder and be more creative in your care solutions. But there is nothing cushy about the loss associated with Alzheimer's – the loss of memory, the loss of rational thought, the loss of judgment, the loss of recognition of others, the loss of self, and often, the loss of dignity. These are the real losses, and they are difficult and heartbreaking in all circumstances.

I'd like to close Diana's story with her words. They are helpful words, insightful words, comforting words:

"Mom's decline has been very gradual and we have had the time to adjust. I have had many times I break down and sob, but have always had my family and friends to turn to. I think being prepared and informed has helped more than I thought. It may be easier for me than my sisters because I am here and get to see her. Also, we have had a wonderful and full life with mom. My mother had a happy childhood, a loving husband, family and friends. Her life was full!!"

3. Alice and Tom's Story

*"I can't remember any time that she got down on the floor
with my daughters, but now she is down on the floor with
my granddaughter."*

~Tom

Finally, in this story, you will gain a son's perspective about drawing closer to his mother, begin to understand the challenges of an unpredictable personality, appreciate the spiritual steps toward providing quality of life, and perhaps identify with the fear, followed by hope, that comes when a parent is diagnosed with Alzheimer's disease.

Tom owns his own very successful law practice. He is a litigator for real estate and construction disputes. He is married, has three daughters, one granddaughter, and two siblings. They all live in close proximity to each other. In fact, his sister works for him and his brother, an estate planner, works in the same building. Tom is in his sixties.

His mother, Alice, also lives in the same area. She is 85 years old and has been widowed twice. In 1990, Tom's father died suddenly of an acute form of leukemia. Alice married again in 2005 to Hugh, a family friend from her younger years. In fact, the original couples played tennis together. When Hugh's wife died, he *"sought Alice out and she closed the deal."* Alice was diagnosed with Alzheimer's disease in 2007. Tom says that he does not know of any history of this disease in his family. He knew all of his grandparents well and they lived into their late 80s and 90s without signs of dementia. Alice is in the moderate stages of Alzheimer's.

Prior to receiving the Alzheimer's diagnosis, Alice displayed symptoms that couldn't be attributed to normal aging. The most prominent symptom was aphasia. Alice lost her ability to communicate with words. The family story was that Alice was the person with all of the words. Tom shares that *"she used to talk all of the time and go off on tangents about all kinds of topics not related to the issue at hand. My dad would have to say 'Alice, bring it back into the conversation.'"* Now, as her children discuss their mother's condition, they say, *"mom used up her words."*

There were other worrisome symptoms. Sometimes, Alice would leave the house in the middle of the night. She would go over to the neighbors in her pajamas. One time, she even ended up in the neighbor's bedroom, and of course, gave them quite a scare.

She would also go through the house and throw away all of the medications in the cupboards. This may have been related to the fact that she had never been one who wanted to take medication. It wasn't a religious conviction against medication, but rather a life-long personal resistance. Yet this behavior seemed out of the norm of reasoned judgment.

Tom thinks back to a time before his mom was remarried. She had a dog and wasn't able to manage taking care of it. Now he realizes that this was probably an earlier symptom of dementia.

Tom's sister Virginia mostly takes care of the medical responsibilities. She took her mother to the general practitioner who referred Alice to a geriatric physician at the University of California, Irvine. It was there that she was diagnosed with Alzheimer's, although the diagnosis wasn't definite. The physician determined that the comprehensive test results indicated that she had symptoms that are consistent with Alzheimer's – so it was the "probable" Alzheimer's diagnosis.

When Tom learned of the diagnosis, he was not surprised, but deeply saddened. Again the diagnosis wasn't definite, it was probable. But there was no other explanation for her symptoms.

With this somewhat vague diagnostic outcome combined with their mother's aphasia, it was very difficult to communicate with her about the disease. The doctor did discuss medications with her, which at first she resisted, consistent with her history of not wanting to take meds. She finally agreed to take them, but Tom says that *"she is on and off about it."*

It was only a year and a half after she had remarried that Alice was diagnosed with Alzheimer's. Before seeking out and marrying Alice, Hugh had just been taking care of a wife with cancer for 20 years. Then in such a short amount of time, *"his new sweetheart got Alzheimer's."* Tom shares that *"Hugh was so very sad, and such a sweet, sweet man."*

As Alice's symptoms got worse, it substantially increased the burden on Hugh. Her children decided that they needed to bring in a caregiver three times a week during the day in order to give her husband a break. Sadly, though, Hugh's health began to fall apart and he went into the hospital in the fall of 2009. As a result, the family went into high gear and got full time care at home. They used an agency that would rotate caregivers through to cover the 24 hours. Until that system was put in place, Tom, his sister, and his brother rotated shifts so that their mom would not be alone.

Hugh never got out of the hospital and subsequent rehabilitation facility. He suffered a fall, and never went home. He died in February of 2010. Alice went to the funeral but Tom isn't sure if she really understood what had happened. She was mostly quiet, sweet and pleasant. She didn't outwardly react to his death. At times since his death, she has said that she misses him. *"Where is that handsome man?"* she would say.

Alice continues to live in her own home with 24-hour in-home care. Some of her caregivers are better than others. Some are particularly attentive. They will get her hair done, take her for a manicure, and even take her to the movies. Sometimes, though, her caregivers aren't careful enough. Alice suffers from lactose intolerance but loves to eat ice cream, which some her caregivers haven't closely monitored. At times, Tom's siblings wondered if their mom was being stretched too much, having even been taken to the caregivers' kids' football games. But Alice seemed to enjoy these outings, so Tom felt that this was giving her joy. He thinks she probably really enjoys that ice cream, too.

Before she had symptoms of Alzheimer's, Alice already had an advance directive in place, so her end-of-life wishes are clear.

Now, Tom says, *"We have had to be very specific with what we want and what we don't want."*

Tom shares:

"The caregivers of the initial agency have not always made decisions that are in my mother's best interests. She has had some intermittent heart issues that are not serious, but for which the caregivers have called 911. This, of course, leads to the emergency room and the hospital, which have been highly upsetting and disorienting for my mom. She was waited up to eight hours to receive attention in the emergency room. She has been admitted to the hospital, consequently suffering from confusion and pain, trying to pull out her IVs, then having her arms restrained to prevent her from succeeding. This has happened four or five times. The quality of her life is already diminished."

Tom knows that in the hospital, it is even worse. He again emphasizes, *"We need to articulate what we don't want."* Tom and his siblings do not want her to go to the hospital.

The family decided that they needed to find caregivers that had better training in providing care for people with Alzheimer's, for their mom. Alice's doctor recommended that they hire a patient advocate through an agency called "Angel *on my shoulder*" to help them research a more effective care solution. The advocate that they hired is a registered nurse and a certified case manager. She has recommended a home health agency that specializes in caring for persons with Alzheimer's as well as specific caregivers within that agency that she believes are especially capable. As I was having this conversation with Tom, his sister was across the way, interviewing a prospective candidate. Their unwavering goal is to keep their mom in her own home with competent and compassionate caregivers.

Tom, Virginia, and Tom's brother Paul have developed, just as my family did, a rather natural division of labor in what they can to offer to their mom. Paul, the estate planner, oversees the finances. His wife does her grocery shopping, making sure that Alice has everything she needs. Virginia has taken on the issues related to medical concerns. She is the key person to interface with the caregiver agency and deals with any problems that arise concerning her mother's daily care needs. And Tom is the spiritual support. He regularly takes his mom to church at St. Mary's Episcopal, where he has become very involved, and assures that she is comfortable and cared for while she is there. Occasionally, Tom and the caregivers take her on Tuesday mornings to a healing service, also at St. Mary's. All three adult children are Alice's social support, taking her out as much as possible, trying to keep her involved in outside activities.

The three siblings, along with Paul's wife, have set up a regular schedule to spend time with their mother and give her a predictable measure of reassurance that she will see one of them four days a week.

Tom's day is Sunday. After taking his mom to church, they go out to brunch. There are two restaurants that are her favorites – where everyone knows her, where they know what she wants. She can point to her selection on the menu. His siblings also have their regular days with specific routines and activities.

However, a problem does arise if they cannot keep to this schedule. Alice gets agitated if they have to make adjustments. Recently, Paul and Virginia had to change their visiting day because they went out of town. They had each been there a day earlier than the set schedule, so Alice expected Tom to be at her home the very next day which was Saturday, not Sunday. She had a horrible day because her days were confused. When Tom came on Sunday, she was so agitated. Tom says, *"She had no idea who I was."*

Tom clearly sees that his mom's symptoms are getting worse. She is starting to have issues with balance and doesn't want to walk. Often, she will just sit around and watch TV. And she now sleeps a lot when the caregivers are there. Tom knows that her children's visits are the most important. He also knows how important it is that all three of her children work together to enhance their mother's well-being. *"I feel like my siblings do so much more; I have a huge practice, three children, a grandchild. I have to find a balance. I couldn't do this alone."* None of them are alone; they are in this together.

Joy, laughter and gratitude are all a part of Tom's experience with his mom. When his daughters were younger, they didn't connect well with their "granny." Alice was absorbed in finding a new husband and didn't reach out to her grandchildren, who were too young to try to develop a good relationship with her. Now, with Alzheimer's, Tom says that, *"She is in love with my kids. She can't express their names, but she expresses love for them. Pretty amazing. And they have been so sweet and kind to her."* Tom's face, as he tells me this, reflects an inner expression of joy.

Tom laughs easily when he shares this story about his mom in church. He says, *"It is cute to see my mom come to church. I sing in the choir so she sits with my wife, or sometimes with the caregiver. My mom doesn't really understand the bulletin and gets a bit confused, but she likes the music and gets into the rhythm of the service. She does go up to the altar for the Eucharist but sometimes she'll try to 'slip the priest some money.' She kneels, opens her hands to receive the bread, and will have cash in her hands to give to the priest."* On my way home from my conversation with Tom, I kept smiling just thinking about this story. What is it about communion that brings so much delight and humor?

Tom feels grateful for his mom's life. Growing up, he was closer to his dad than to his mom. Now he has grown a lot closer to her through this illness, feeling great compassion toward her.

And he also feels grateful that his daughters are now close to their granny. Alice also takes joy in her great granddaughter. Tom says, **"I can't remember any time that she got down on the floor with my daughters, but now she is down on the floor with my granddaughter."**

With Alzheimer's disease, the good parts of Alice's personality have gotten better, the bad parts have gotten worse. On the one hand, she acts more kindly and more gently than she had ever been before. Prior to her illness, she was not the sweet person that she has now become.

However, she does get agitated which brings out hostile behavior, especially when she receives personal care. She can be quite hostile to the caregivers when they give her a bath. In the family, Tom's sister bears the brunt of their mother's agitation because she is the one taking her to the doctor and trying to facilitate good physical care for her. Tom remembers that during his childhood and into adulthood, his mom did have this mean side to her. Now that behavior is exacerbated.

Currently, Alice has a new caregiver but seems to be increasingly agitated. Tom thinks this may be because this particular caregiver, who actually is from the new agency that was recommended to them, is more direct with her instructions to Alice and doesn't take no for an answer. The family continues to watch closely to see if their mom will adjust to this different approach, and if this situation will turn around and resolve.

Tom feels like his family is doing "OK" as they provide care and support for their mom. He, Virginia and Paul are all regularly talking to each other and problem solve well together; they all work in the same building so communication is easy. Their decision to hire the patient advocate was a great idea.

Their mom's abilities continue to decline, though. It's getting harder for her to walk. It is getting harder to take her to her favorite restaurants because she has difficulty going to and managing the bathroom. Her last hospitalization brought her down a notch, and it is becoming more challenging to communicate with her.

Tom shares, *"I personally struggle with having a conversation. It's one-sided, so it's hard for me to talk with her."* He talks to her about what the kids are doing and she seems to understand. She used to be interested in the extensive construction going on at his place of business, but that conversation doesn't capture her anymore. Tom doesn't talk about work with her, but says he doesn't talk much to anyone about his work. *"Why it is so awkward between mom and me is that I have always been a better listener. She used to do all of the talking."* Tom says he is a *"person of few words."*

Alice does still have interests, though. She likes to watch sports on TV. She loves to go to her granddaughter's performances in musical theater, provided the show doesn't last too long. And, she still recognizes her family and enjoys her children's visits.

When Tom and his siblings are discussing their mom, they often get choked up. They are already grieving for her, for all of the individual ways that she is already gone. *"I don't want to watch her spiral down anymore,"* says Tom. *"It's so sad. I just want her to go suddenly without pain. There will be sadness when she passes, but there will be relief more than anything ... I think we are all taking this day by day ... I hope mom doesn't go on and on, but if she does, then we will deal with it."*

Tom's advice to other adult children who have a parent that has been diagnosed with Alzheimer's is both practical and personal.

From a practical perspective, Tom highly recommends hiring a patient advocate (also called a care manager or an aging life professional) as his family did, to help develop the best plan of care. The advocate is highly trained in issues relating to dementia and has knowledge of resources that the family may not find on its own. The fee for an advocate is reasonable and a family can utilize the services of the advocate as much or as little as desired.

Since Tom and his siblings are unanimous in wanting to keep their mom at home, the advocate has been vital to that plan. She has kept them from making big mistakes. Not only has she provided them with a care plan and connected them to resources, she has also brought in new and creative ideas. The advocate arranged for a massage therapist. She suggested an Episcopal healer, who comes to Alice's home, lays hands on her and prays. This broad range of resources and services has improved her quality of life.

On a personal level, Tom thoughtfully advises, *"Just be present for your parent in the best way that you can be present. That is so meaningful for mom, and it makes this time more joyful."*

Tom admits to a certain amount of fear for his own life and aging process because of this Alzheimer's journey with his mother. He has been pretty healthy in his attitude about growing old and dying. He's not afraid of that. But now he does fear *"losing it while I'm still alive."* He knows how hard it is to watch the mental decline of his mom; he doesn't want his kids to watch him go down that same road of slowly increasing confusion. As we all would prefer, Tom would like to just die suddenly one day. Now he says that *"fear is present for the first time."*

This fear has, however, created a new awareness within Tom. As he so beautifully says, it has *"brought to my soul the need to live as well as we can; let the people we know and love know that we do love them- let them know that."* Tom leads a very busy life. Sometimes he gets caught up in *"other stuff"* and forgets to express his love. But he is trying; he is trying every day.

It is only with help and support that an adult child can deal with the heartbreak of a parent with Alzheimer's disease. For Tom, the close connection to his siblings has helped him the most. They have planned together, made decisions together, and given each other the freedom to get "choked-up" as they already grieve for their mother.

Tom has also found great support from the members of his church community. They care about him; they care about his mom. They ask about her and offer their encouragement. *"It is a wonderful community."*

And Tom has the great pleasure of watching his daughters and his mom interact with love and kindness – a growing relationship that helps him to replace his fear and sadness with hope and joy.

Key Learning Writing and Reflection Points

So what do these stories tell us – Diana's story, Tom's story, my story?

They do tell us that Alzheimer's disease is a heartbreaking diagnosis. The three of us have all watched our mothers slowly fade away from us. Whether our parent is in the "hostile" group or the "happy" group makes a difference only for the moment, not for the long term. The loss of who our parent once was creates a sad and difficult path to walk as we desperately hang on to our parent-child relationship, even when that parent is no longer sure who we are.

These stories speak to the absolute necessity of seeking help and support from family, from friends, from professionals. Only with this support can realistic goals be established, with shared responsibility and shared decision-making.

Each story, in its own unique way, emphasizes the importance of getting a diagnosis, planning, preparing, seeking out resources, and trying different strategies while simultaneously coping with the disease one day at a time.

Every situation is different. For my mother, she no longer connected with her own home and the burden to try to keep her there was overwhelming. A familiar Lutheran assisted living and nursing care community became the best option. For Diana's mom, 24-hour in-home care worked well until her struggle with congestive heart failure was too disruptive. Then a carefully selected Alzheimer's facility was determined to best meet her needs. For Tom's mom, the whole family lives in the same area so they are committed to keeping her in her own home throughout this Alzheimer's journey.

These stories tell us that Alzheimer's is not only a heartbreaking diagnosis, it is a frightening diagnosis. We are afraid for what our parent is going to have to endure, probably for a very long time; we are afraid for our own prospects of inheriting a disease that robs us of who we are. I find myself worrying when I am awake in the middle of the night that I hope I have grandchildren before I won't know who they are. My mother started to display some confusion in her early seventies. I am already in my sixties and none of my adult children are planning to get married any time soon. Will I know my grandchildren? I don't know.

The positive side of this fear is that it generates healthier living, motivating us to nurture our physical, mental, emotional and spiritual well-being. Alice Park, in her cover story in Time Magazine on Alzheimer's (October 25, 2010), says that, *"Living robustly and well is one of the best weapons we have against the disease – at least until science's heavier artillery is finally ready to be wheeled into place."* Indeed, the most current research indicates that social engagement, physical exercise, cognitive fitness activities, and good sleep habits may slow down the progression of the disease and add years of a good quality of life. There is a recent study that shows a marked improvement in brain scans as a result of regular cardiovascular exercise. This is very hopeful!

Perhaps the most important lesson of our stories is that even with the heartbreak, the care challenges, and the fear that Alzheimer's disease brings into our lives – it is possible to find moments of joy, reasons to laugh, and the strength to be grateful that we have the honor to help our parent as life is slowly coming to an end. It is possible to hang on to fond memories that will sustain us and make us smile as we remember the good times with our parents that have, in large part, made us who we are. *Nothing, not even Alzheimer's disease, can take that away.*

7

Grieving for Our Parents

— ❤ —

"My mother and father were always so enthusiastic about accomplishments in life. Not being able to share these is the biggest thing that I miss."

~Mike

"Nothing prepared me for the finality of my mother's death – a profound sense of sadness and the loss of someone I'd loved, who'd loved me, unconditionally, my entire life. Her death ended the longest 'role' and biggest chapter of my life . . . I was no longer someone's daughter."

~Patsy

*W*hen I was writing the chapter on humor, I kept laughing, sometimes just within, and sometimes out loud. That warped sense of humor just kept emerging. Now as I write about grief, I am sad, and my eyes are teary. I may have to stop at times and have a good cry. My dad died in 1989 and my mom in 2002 – and I still grieve for them – not all day or every day – but I do still grieve for them. I especially miss my dad who was the rock of our family. You never fully get over losing a parent.

As we move through this chapter, some of our Cast will share experiences with losing their parents. Of course, the stories will evoke some feelings of sadness. However, as the Cast share specific coping mechanisms for thinking about and managing grief, you will also discover elements of inspiration, acceptance and ways to find peace.

When my dad died, he was relatively young at 71. What had started as "something small, probably a urinary tract infection that can be managed" became, through a series of tests "just to be sure," prostate cancer that had already spread to the bone. With each phone call from my dad to let me know the results of the latest test, my heart sank a little lower. My stomach took another sharp twist. My chest got tighter. And the tears that come even now as I write this began. The cancer had spread throughout his entire skeletal system, and I cried, *"I can't imagine this world without my dad in it. I can't imagine my life without him."* I didn't believe that I could ever feel truly happy again.

Losing a parent is HUGE. Yes, it is the proper order of things – our parents surely are supposed to die before we do. That doesn't mean, though, that it is easy to accept the death of a parent. Nor does it mean that after a few months, we should just get over it and not talk to people about it anymore. After all, we have known our parents throughout our entire lives. They have loved us, nurtured us, supported us, bugged us, disciplined us, criticized us, and commented on the pros and cons of our life journey so far – perhaps more than we wanted. But in the end, if we were among the many lucky ones, we know that through all of the ups and downs of our relationship and of our life, they have loved us wholly and unconditionally.

The Tsunami

Grief has been described as being a tsunami – it comes in waves and can be unpredictable. Sometimes the waves totally wash over you and you will feel overwhelmingly sad. Sometimes just the ripples surface, and you become teary over a song or a certain favorite place. As time passes, the waves become less frequent and less intense, but unlike a tsunami they never go away altogether. After her parents died, Dawn embraced this metaphor about grieving because it helped her to realize that there was nothing wrong with her when *"a familiar song that reminded me of my parents would bring me to tears."*

Patsy also experiences her grief in unpredictable waves that she describes as *"full of twists and turns."* She shares, *"I would think that I was handling things OK, and then I would see a particular photo or memento or my sister would use an expression that sounded like my mom . . . and suddenly a wave of sadness would wash over me, one that I could physically feel, and I'd need to excuse myself and sit down and perhaps shed some tears."* Experiencing these waves of sadness, at times, for the rest of our own adult lives is a completely normal and healthy way to express our grief over losing our parents. But for most of us, the waves become gentler over time.

After your parent's funeral or memorial service is over, the food provided by friends is long gone, the cards have been read multiple times and set aside, and everyone has moved on – the reality sets in. Perhaps days, weeks, or months have passed when it hits you that you will never see your parent again, at least not in this life, the life that we know and touch and feel. You will want to call your mom and share about an important accomplishment in your own life – you may even actually pick up the phone to call, only to suddenly remember that she is not there. *Drowning waves of sadness.*

Or you long for some words of wisdom from your dad or maybe just a huge hug because something difficult or sad has happened in your family. You suddenly feel very alone because you know he cannot help you or hold you. My sister Gaynelle, when she is discouraged about some decisions that are being made at the school where she has taught for over 40 years, says, *"This is when I just want to put my head on Dad's shoulder and have him tell me that everything will be OK." Nostalgic waves of sadness.*

When my daughter, at 21 years old, was diagnosed with thyroid cancer, I was painfully reminded of how much I, too, still long for my dad's words of reassurance. Even though her prognosis was excellent, the situation was still frightening and overwhelming. I needed to hear my dad's comforting voice. No one else could provide that for me. No one can take his place. *Gentle, yet longing, waves of sadness.*

I don't think we realize how often, as adults, we turned to our parents to share the good, get help with the bad, or to just try to sort things out – until they are gone. And they may have been gone for many, many years. We still want their comfort and maybe even some advice. And so we experience these sometimes strong, and sometimes gentle, waves of sadness.

Feelings of Relief

You may experience feelings of relief when your parent dies. This is especially true when there has been a long chronic illness that has caused pain, suffering and often confusion. Patsy felt a profound sense of sadness, yet relief, over the finality of her mother's death, even though her condition had been deteriorating for years. Patsy says that she *"knew where things were progressing to. There was an odd sense of relief in knowing that she had been freed from a body that was no longer functioning. My religious beliefs helped me think of her soul ascending to heaven – I even laughed at the vision of my dad, my oldest sister, and my grandmother greeting her warmly with her favorite drink as she entered the Pearly Gates."*

Mike's father had health problems from age 52 to 85. *"He had become more and more restricted, and his basic human dignity was gone. I am angry about that and sad about that. So at the end, when he did pass away, there was a sense of relief, of peace – but obviously you regret losing your parents."*

Dawn's parents had both struggled with their health over many years, into their nineties, hung in there for each other, and died within four months of each other. *"I did feel a sense of relief when my parents died. I thought, finally this is over. They had suffered so many losses and experienced so many indignities. I sometimes thought, how long will this go on? My dad went from being so vibrant and capable to having someone change his diapers."*

I know that I certainly felt a sense of relief myself when my mother died. She had been suffering from Alzheimer's disease for over seven years and had been in skilled nursing care, not knowing any of her family, for two years. It seemed as though she would go on like that forever. Yet, when she took a definite downward turn, she died within three days. It was a relief for all of our family.

Maybe feeling relief seems a bit selfish, but I completely believe that my mom would never have wanted to be living in the condition she was in. Mom would have been mortified if she had been aware that she said cruel things, that she didn't know us, that her physical body required care 24 hours a day. I often thought, then, about how private and modest she had always been, and how nursing care would have been the ultimate embarrassment for her.

I also believe that although Mom wasn't cognitively aware of her overall condition, she knew deep inside that something terrible was wrong – she was angry, she was sad, she was suffering. So yes – her death, at first, was a relief. And to feel relief is a normal, understandable reaction to a parent's long journey of decline. Don't be surprised by it or feel guilty about it. Relief can allow us to breathe again.

Anticipatory Grief

Some members of our Cast share about the experience of anticipatory grief. When there is a long, chronic, physical illness or a slow cognitive decline into advancing dementia, you may naturally grieve along the way, with each change, with each loss. Since

Mike's father had suffered health problems related to multiple sclerosis for over 30 years, Mike tells us that, *"I did some grieving prior to his death – I had a father who was very successful, a surgeon, a good guy, a loving father – to have so much removed from his life for such a long period of time – I felt frustration and overall sadness. The grieving process for my father was going on for a long time."*

Patsy had grieved sporadically over the years as her mother's condition deteriorated. She shares, *"Each time dementia robbed her of an ability or some portion of her memory, each time she 'dropped' to a lower plateau in her quality of life, I grieved that loss and cursed the disease."*

I had that same experience of anticipatory grief with my mom. During the time that she was sinking deeper into the confusion of Alzheimer's, there was a major earthquake in Southern California. Mom was alone, in her bed, when it struck at 6:00 a.m. She never was able to recover to her previous level of cognitive ability after that traumatic event. She dropped to a lower level of functioning, a lower plateau. I grieved the loss of her capacity.

Not too many years later, my older sister had a serious heart attack. This event catapulted my mother way into the past and she kept referring to my sister as "her baby." She couldn't understand where we were in time. She lost another hold on her mental and emotional well-being. I grieved. I cried.

You may currently be in this stage of anticipatory grief. If you are, please reach out to others who are also anticipating the death of a parent — perhaps your siblings or a close friend. Or talk with someone that you know whose parent's death resulted from a long, chronic illness or who lost a parent in recent years. Remember, other people want to help. Sharing these feelings with others who have had a similar experience will give meaning to this anticipatory grief. And it may help to lessen the pain of the grief that is still to come.

Finality

The finality of a parent's death hits hard. This holds true even if we have already grieved for some of the losses. It hits hard even if we are relieved at the moment of death. The finality is almost shocking and terribly sad even if we think that we are prepared for the death of a parent. Patsy tells us that, **"nothing prepared me for the finality of my mother's death – a profound sense of sadness and the loss of someone I'd loved, who'd loved me, unconditionally, my entire life. Her death ended the longest 'role' and biggest chapter of my life . . . I was no longer someone's daughter."**

Patsy continues, speaking of her father this time: "*When my dad died many years earlier, it was rather sudden – he'd had heart problems, went in for open heart surgery to correct the problems, but did not recover and died within about a week. I thought it was the suddenness of it that made it so hard to get over – but I've learned that, sudden or not, prepared or not, losing a parent brings on an intense feeling of loss, grief, sadness and disorientation that is hard to bear.*"

Searching for Peace

How do we get from this place of sadness, of overwhelming loss, to at least a certain amount of acceptance and a sense of peace? Dawn knows about peace. She shares, *"I did feel a sense of peace when my parents died. It was past their time. My parents were so close and had to be together. In the nursing home, they put their beds together so that they could hold hands at night."*

We can take small steps to healing and peace along many different paths. Let's explore some of these steps that may lead us to pathways of healing.

Services Comfort Us

The service itself – funeral, memorial, graveside, spreading of ashes – not always, but for many people, is the beginning of the healing process. It can be a gathering of family and friends, a tribute to the person who died, a celebration of his or her life. Healing can begin through a formal tradition or ritual of saying good-bye.

Dawn had a memorial service for both her mom and dad at the nursing home, just for family, staff and other residents. She remembers, *"My dad didn't want any service, so originally for him [he had died four months previously], I had family over and we shared about him, but it felt awkward and not so meaningful. The service for my mom gave me closure – I did this for my mom and then kind of rolled my dad into it. I wore a bright red suit that my mom, even in later stages of dementia, always recognized and liked. I thought, with a lighter heart, 'My mom will see me.'"*

Six months after his mother died in Los Angeles, Peter and his wife took her ashes up north to Lake Tahoe, where his original family home was located. They called it the "Tupperware to Tahoe trip." *"All along the way, we left some ashes in her favorite places,"* he says. *"Then we went to our old house, flooded with memories and emotions, and we put the rest of her ashes around the trees that she had planted. I felt such a joy and relief – the sorrow was turned into a belief that I will see my parents again one day."*

My husband's father died the day after Thanksgiving 2009. He was 92 years old. Yet, even at that age, having out-lived most of his long-time friends, his memorial service was full of people. There was family, of course, which included my mother-in-law, three adult children, and seven grandchildren; friends and colleagues of the adult children; a few long-time friends; and several people from the retirement home where my husband's parents had lived for the past two years. The pastor took the time to learn a lot about my father-in-law so that his message was personal and meaningful. My husband did the eulogy, which included stories that highlighted his dad's very distinctive characteristics. We nodded in agreement, we laughed, and we cried. The last year of my father-in-law's life had been very difficult with strokes, broken bones, hospital, rehab, nursing home – so this service, if it could say something, would say, "Let the healing begin." It was wonderful and he would have enjoyed it!

Time and Self-Help

A good send-off, so to speak, can lay the groundwork for healthy grieving and coming to terms with the loss of a parent. But it is only the beginning. We have lived our whole life with the presence of our parents. The loss becomes more real with the passing of time.

Time is always said to be the great healer – or if it doesn't heal, *"Time does help, as the wound doesn't feel so fresh,"* says Patsy. But as we wait for time to lessen the pain of loss, there are ways to promote our own healing.

One way to help with our own healing is to just let ourselves *feel the feelings of sadness and loss* when they hit us and not fight them. I remember a few years after my father died of prostate cancer I was sitting in a board of directors meeting. The CEO announced that he would be taking time off and possibly retiring because he had prostate cancer. I had known this person for quite some time, but my reaction was as though it was my own father telling me this. The CEO's announcement immediately brought back that moment when my dad told us that he had this cancer. My eyes welled up with tears, and I excused myself to the bathroom and let myself weep. With the miracle of soothing, "redness-relief" eye drops and good makeup, I was later able to return to the meeting and participate in a coherent way. But everyone somehow knew I had been crying.

I probably could have fought off those tears and managed to pay at least some attention to the meeting's agenda. However, I needed to have that good cry – for my dad, and for the CEO who was facing this same disease. There wasn't a single person in that boardroom that made me feel that what I did was inappropriate or weak – and they were all men! Most knew my dad's history and were aware that I had known this CEO for a long time. The meeting just went on. It was OK. I was OK.

So we need to let ourselves cry when that wave of sadness hits. Of if you are not a crier (as some of you probably are not), you may just need to sit alone and think about that sad memory until you are ready to let it go in that moment. It may not always be convenient but you may still have to take some private time. Patsy says, *"We have to let those waves pass through. They DO move along, though sometimes not so quickly."*

Taking Care of Business

For some people, it helps to take care of the "business stuff" surrounding the death of a parent. Patsy knew that her mother's style would have been not to procrastinate and to take care of financial matters, respond to calls and kindnesses, and start to deal with material items left behind – so that is what she did following her mother's death. Doing these things as her mother would have done them was a way of honoring her and starting to deal with the loss. *"Sometimes I'd busy myself with the details that followed her death – the paperwork, sorting things out, closing accounts, etc. – I think it helped me feel closer to her, as if at least I was doing something to help."* The key here was that she really let herself pay attention to these things and experienced them enveloped in thoughts and memories of her mother. It became part of her grieving process.

It can also be true that taking care of "business stuff" gets in the way of grieving. I have known people who, immediately following a parent's death, become mechanically involved in sorting through things, throwing things away (sometimes regretting it later), putting things away, filing things away, etc., and they didn't allow themselves to feel grief. This is a way of staying active, focused on "stuff," immune to sadness or pain. That is not necessarily unhealthy at first, because it can get you through those initial days or weeks that are almost unbearable.

I, myself, got very wrapped up in writing the program for my dad's funeral service. That got me through the service quite well. I was focused on how it was all going to go. Would the service be good enough to fully honor this amazing and accomplished man – my dad? Did the choir have enough time to practice? Was the picture on the front of the program the best possible portrayal of my dad?

A problem can develop if this "dealing with stuff" behavior lasts so long that it defers the grief to a much later time, or covers the grief up altogether. In that case, the grief will still be there. It is trying to bubble up to the surface, trying to form a wave to wash over you. There is no timetable for when grieving should start or stop. We are all different in how we handle life's sorrows. But if you have not allowed those waves to wash over you, you may begin to experience physical symptoms, such as headaches, stomach problems or depression. You may overreact to small disappointments with anger or excessive tears. Grief will not go away. You must experience it. For the great majority of us, allowing grief to wash over us, to let ourselves tear up and cry, to share about and clearly remember our parents will lead us eventually to that peaceful place in which grief is not quite so painful.

Talking Openly about the Parent You Lost

On that last point, those I interviewed who had lost one or both parents said it was essential to talk about the parent who died as a way to express grief and understand it. I strongly agree! Dawn says, "*What was helpful to me was to talk to other people about my parents, share their story, and get advice from others who had grieved for their parents.*"

Sometimes I think people are afraid to have these conversations, especially within the family, because it will make everyone sad. That is true. It may make everyone sad. That is the point. And in feeling sad, grief will start to lessen just a bit. If you still have one parent, share with that parent your good memories about the loved one you have both lost. It is good to get together with family, look at pictures, share stories, even share about past problems, and for each person to remember how that parent was an integral part of the family story. Patsy shares that, "*The first year after my mother's death, we got through every key holiday and birthday by talking about her and realizing that we could celebrate even though she was gone.*"

And don't hesitate to talk about the loss with friends, even if they have not experienced the death of a parent and think you should be over it by now. They will someday have their turn, and your example of sharing freely and openly about grieving will help them immensely.

My family, of Norwegian stock, isn't always the best at sharing emotions and sadness. The stoic stereotype fits our family quite well. We have a very special Christmas Eve tradition, which had always involved my dad reading the Christmas story in his deep, warm, pastoral "Lutheran bishop" voice. He was the heart of our Christmas Eve. Yet, after his death, it took us five years to really openly acknowledge that he wasn't there anymore. I think we were afraid to allow sadness into our tradition. We were afraid that it would be too sad for my mom. My nephew would read the Christmas story. We sang carols. Family members shared their most recent talent. We played silly games. And we opened presents. But we didn't talk about my dad. Then Christmas Eve morning of 1994, I decided to write a poem about him and share it as my part of the program. That poem opened the door to all kinds of emotion – sadness, yes, but joy and laughter in the memories, too—and it brought my dad back into the Christmas Eve tradition.

We learned from that experience. When my mother died, she still participated in Christmas Eve through us, through the memories that we shared about her. To this day, we always pause and remark that my brother is doing my mom's part by playing the piano for the carols and leading us in the opening prayer.

Visiting Favorite Places

As time passes, you may discover that it is comforting to visit areas where you spent time with your parents – favorite shared places. Patsy says that at first she avoided spots that her mom loved, but that deprived her of enjoying locations that they had shared, places that had lots of good memories. Mike and his family go to his parents' favorite vacation destination – the Mauna Kea Beach Hotel in Kona, Hawaii. They pose for pictures in exactly the same spaces that his parents did with exactly the same pose. *"When my mom was there, it was the happiest days of her life, and when I go there, it's the happiest time for me."*

Visiting these favorite locales is also a way to share more about your parents with your own children. Your children (young adults probably) may have memories of a long illness, dementia, pain and death when they think about their grandparents. How wonderful for them to go to fun destinations, and learn about what their grandparents enjoyed when they were healthy and vibrant. You can create new memories with your own children as you revisit memories that your parents created with you. These are the times that make it possible to smile as we remember.

Writing about Them & Our Experience of Loss

Still another way to express, and possibly lessen our grief, is to write about the parent who has died. This might be through our own personal journaling, writing down our memories, our feelings, our longings. Or it may be through written communications with others, sharing with them what it is that we are experiencing.

It may be something as simple as the poem that I wrote about my dad for our Christmas Eve program. It may even take the form of an entire article or story. For Patsy, it was writing her mother's obituary. She shares, *"Writing an obituary was hard but reminded me of how much my mother meant to so many people over her 87 years."*

When her mom was in the last weeks of life, Ellis sent her family and friends a series of emails that beautifully, painfully, yet with some humor, described her mother's dying process. She recorded how the family responded, in the midst of their tears, to support her and honor her wishes. You can only know the value and depth of this communication by reading what Ellis composed. The day after her mother's death, Ellis wrote the following:

> *My mother died as she lived ... with gratitude and appreciation. She managed to give all her caregivers a kiss and hug, and thanked them for their kindness. She apologized for being a burden ... which she certainly wasn't. In the end, she kept her eyes open when family members were in the room and managed to hug and kiss the neighbors and friends who came by to say their good-byes. She had music in the background, some of her favorites – Perry Como –"Papa Loves Mambo." The last few days were very tough ... she was breathing very hard and squeezed our hands. It was difficult to witness. We gave her permission to go, and told her that we would take care of Pop. But she was reluctant ... I think she wanted to do it on her terms and nobody was going to tell her differently ... this would be in character of who she was. I know many of you have lost loved ones, and that this journey is never easy and is different for each one of us. I am grateful we experienced some of our bereavement prior to her death. Waiting for death is hard ... your whole sense of time changes ... a day is a week, a week a year. We were grateful for the time, but*

also looking forward to the end of strife and the beginning of peace.

What a privilege it was to receive these words from this courageous woman! Through her words, Ellis captures her mother's life-long uniqueness. She expresses both the beauty and the agony of the dying process, and offers a sense of comfort to others and to herself with a promise of peace. The written word is a permanent place to express and share our grief.

Moving Forward

The most honorable way to remember our parents and celebrate their lives is to learn from them, in life and in death. Equally important is to act on what we have learned and change our own life in ways that benefit our physical, mental and emotional well-being. And we need to share with others about our grieving process in order to encourage, support and affirm. How exactly do we do that? *Listen to* the following answers to my questions.

Question: In what ways did the death of your parent(s) affect how you live now?

For Mike, it was a change in how he chose to live: *"I quit my high stress job about six months after my mother passed away. With my mom, I relived my dad's death . . . it is a different feeling when you have lost both of them – the level of sadness was greater, because I grouped it together . . . I was twice as sad. It changed my life – I was tired of what I was doing, the people, the place – life is too short. I finally did what my mother said to me for 35 years. I stopped and smelled the roses. My parents' passing had a profound effect on my life. I was going to do what I wanted to do and not do what I don't want to do. I spend more time with my wife. Now my girls have careers and the cycle is starting again. Part of grief is also a reminder of your own mortality."*

Patsy, who "loves to learn," continues in her quest for learning as she remembers her parents' lives. She adopted good financial planning skills, inspired by her parents. She says, *"They both came from poor farming families, but were smart, had a strong work ethic, and weren't afraid to pick up and move – even with five kids! They worked hard, saved, invested money, and provided a comfortable life for our family. Even in their later years, and even with my mother's dementia and needing years of full-time care, my parents had built a nest egg that lasted throughout their lives. They even left a little money for us kids and the grandkids – an awesome legacy."* Patsy recognizes what a great example her parents set for her!

Patsy also went through the rather laborious and *"bothersome"* process of helping her mother set up a living trust. She notes, *"After her death, I appreciated that things were in very good order and realized how smart she was to have things spelled out clearly. I hope to be equally effective."*

After watching her very smart, capable mother get older and struggle with limited mobility and become confused at simple things, Patsy is much more aware of older adults who may need some assistance. *"It's like my personal radar is better tuned to recognize such situations and offer assistance,"* she says. *"I see the confused older lady in the grocery store or the older woman that just can't keep standing in a long line . . . and I find myself approaching that person to see if I can help. It feels good and oddly familiar, and I find it makes me feel closer to the memory of my parents . . . like I'm sort of helping my parents, or applying something I learned from them."*

Patsy continues, *"My interest in genealogy and wanting to get information from older relatives is in part spurred by the fact that I didn't learn what I could have about family history from my parents. I wasted that opportunity but it has encouraged me to be more intentional with other relatives to learn about their family history."*

This is an area that many of you may want to underscore. I know there are many things that I would like to ask my parents now that I never took the time to ask. I don't even know why. We all get so busy building our own lives and families, but our parents' history is an important piece of who we are and how we live our lives. If you are fortunate and your parents are living, take the time to ask questions and record their stories. You may learn to understand yourself better. And you will certainly know your parents better!

For Dawn, the death of her parents allows her to feel "more free" as she lives her life today. *"When my parents were ill, we couldn't go overseas for any extended period (my husband had some offers), but I was an only child and I had to stay close. We can have more adventures now – we may even join the Peace Corps. My parents would like that."* As an only child, Dawn was tied to parent care responsibilities for years. She fulfilled these responsibilities with love and devotion. Now she can enjoy this freedom. And when she thinks and dreams about her parents, *"They are healthy again."*

Question: What emotions arise now, after time has passed, when thinking about your parents?

When I asked our Cast this question, the feelings that unfolded again tell of the strong desire to still share life with their parents – sharing joys and accomplishments about themselves and about grandchildren, getting advice, longing for their wisdom.

Patsy wants to have one more good conversation about business, stocks and real estate with her dad. She would like her parents to be at graduations, know about job promotions, and be there for other events that would have been meaningful for them. She wishes that her parents could have continued to be a part of her son's life so that he would have had the grandparent experience. Her dad and her son would have been able to enjoy a shared passion for golf.

Dawn thinks about how fun it would be for her parents to come to her new home in Lake Havasu (she and her husband have now retired), share in the lives of their grandchildren, and enjoy their great-grandchildren. *"I miss having parents – I can't share accomplishments with them – I always wanted to make them proud. Little things make me think of them. There is an oil painting of a red barn that my dad painted that now hangs in the social service office of the facility where my parents lived at the end of their lives. It makes me so happy that someone loves that painting."*

Mike wants to be able to call his dad when he has a health problem so that his dad can tell him that it is nothing to worry about. But the biggest thing that he misses, just like Patsy and Dawn, and probably like most of us who have lost our parents, is not being able to share life successes with his parents. **"My mother and father were always so enthusiastic about accomplishments in life,"** Mike says. **"Not being able to share these is the biggest thing that I miss."**

Certainly, there is a strong element of sadness when we wish for our parents to still be a part of what we are doing today. Even so, it can also be uplifting to think of them in an active, vital way – what they would say, do or think about what is going on now. It somehow brings them back to life for us and helps us to remember what they did say, do or think when they were healthy, involved in life, involved with us. I believe this opens us up to the positive memories – and those positive memories will begin to outweigh the sad, grieving and tearful times.

Question: What do we say, those of us who have lost our parents some time ago, to those who have recently lost a parent?

Dawn says, *"I would share about the tsunami effect of grief; that it comes and goes in waves. Also, I would tell someone to know who their sounding board is—someone who will just be there and listen without comment."*

And Patsy simply says, *"It is SOOOO important to acknowledge to the person that you are sorry for what they are going through, and express support. No matter how hard it is to say those words, I believe people need to hear that!"*

And I say, along with Patsy, that probably the most important thing that we "experienced grievers" need to say, very simply, is how sorry we truly are about the death of someone's parent – expressing that wholeheartedly and without reservation. Then we need to be ready to listen, comfort and support.

For many of us, it is difficult to just say, "I'm sorry" and then listen. We want to give extra comfort. We want to say something more. This is always well intended but often is not helpful. We will offer phrases such as, "Your father is in a better place now," "Now your mother is whole again and at rest," or, "This is all part of God's greater plan." Since my father was a pastor and bishop, I was inundated with these spiritual, well-meaning expressions of sympathy. They didn't help, not when his death was so raw.

While these are nice things to say, they don't respect the sorrow of the actual heartbreaking loss in this physical world that we currently know. They almost deny it. This is not to say that at some point in the grieving process, especially for those with a religious/spiritual understanding, these phrases may not be comforting and helpful. I don't intend to demean them. But at the time of loss, a simple heartfelt "I'm sorry" or "I am here for you" speaks to the immediate loss. Then we can go on to accept however it is that our friend needs to grieve, be a sounding board and listen without comment, begin to understand what they need to hear, and hold our friend tightly when the waves of sadness threaten to drown the person that we care about. Others will do the same for us.

Closing Thoughts on Grief

Perhaps the most difficult issue about grief is the unsettling nature of the future without our parents. What should we expect as we travel the long and winding path of grief?

I say, don't expect anything – because there are no "shoulds" or "shouldn'ts" when it comes to grieving. There is only you, and your way of grieving for your parent.

However, there are some things that you "can" know.

You can know that even if you are relieved at the time of death because it is finally the end of suffering, you are not cold or insensitive. It is probably the end of some pretty difficult, yet dedicated caregiving. It means that you loved your parent, you have done your best, and that peace will eventually come.

You can know that sometimes your grief may take on an unexpected dimension. You may find yourself crying when you least expect it. You may suddenly be laughing at some memory that you didn't think was funny at the time. Or maybe you did, but didn't know that you could still laugh.

Months or years later, you may feel as though your parent just died yesterday – those everlasting waves of sadness.

You can know that friends have experienced their own grief for their parents or are now struggling with end-of-life issues. You can share with them, let them be your sounding board, and do the same for them in return.

And you can know, almost with certainty, that with time, the good and happy memories will outweigh the difficult and sad memories. Even though you never fully get over losing your parents, you will come to understand that the best of your parents is living within you. And your efforts to continue this legacy of "their best" are a brilliant reflection of your gratitude to them.

Personal Epilogue

There are days now when I don't think about my dad. So many years have passed and life has gone on. But when I have something important to consider or am facing a critical situation, such as my daughter's illness, I still ask myself what he would have said. I can almost hear his voice. I feel comforted. That is when I remember how very lucky I am to have had such a wonderful father and hope that I have some of him in me. Then I wish that I could go into his study, interrupt his work, and have a good chat.

Key Learning Points

- Grief for a parent is multi-faceted and can reveal itself in anticipatory grief, feelings of relief, a shocking finality and on-going waves of sadness.

- It is essential to recognize, express and honor our grief so that we do not experience negative physical, mental and emotional symptoms within our own life's journey.

- After the loss of our parents, we can begin to find peace through meaningful family traditions, embracing the positives that we have learned from our parents, openly sharing and writing about them, visiting some of their favorite places, and celebrating how the "best of them" is a "part of us."

Time for Writing and Reflection

1. **For Adult Children with Living Parents:** Think of at least five questions that explore unfamiliar, yet important aspects of your parents' life – past, present and future. The follow-up, of course, is to sit with your parents, listen to their answers/stories, and possibly record or write down the responses—either during one conversation or over time.

2. **For Those Who Have Lost a Parent:** Select your favorite memory of the parent who has died. Write about this memory in detail and share it with your living parent, with siblings, with friends and with your children. Let joy, sorrow, laughter and tears overflow.

3. **For All Adult Children:** Write a short story, poem or journal entry that celebrates the many struggles and accomplishments in the lives of one or both of your parents.

8

Closing Thoughts on Aging Parents: Reccommendations From Our Cast to You

"Research . . . Share . . . Listen . . . Forgive . . . Celebrate"

~Collective Wisdom

*A*s you learned in the opening section on our Cast of "Character," the adult children that I interviewed for this book were not randomly selected. Rather, I very intentionally selected people who have dedicated hours, days, months and years to spending time with their aging parents, to providing care for their aging parents, and to sharing with others about the challenges of this time in their lives. Some had good relationships with their parents, others did not. Some had strong family support, others did not. Some had easy access to resources, others did not. Their common thread was, very simply, their dedication to their aging parents.

These are the voices of those who have walked alongside their aging parents on a rather long path with joy, sorrow, success, failure, laughter, tears, resentment and gratitude. From these voices, if you have listened carefully, hopefully you've gained knowledge, developed new insight, and grabbed on to the courage and hope that you need to successfully navigate your own journey with your aging parents.

In summary, then, from Act I, I share the collective wisdom of adult children who have thought deeply about their experiences with their parents and are willing to honestly share their stories. This is what they - and I - recommend.

About Resources

- Remember that your parents may be your greatest resource. Ask them what they want, how they feel, how they want to live their final years.

- Plan ahead for the changes that will come as your parents age. Read about aging (Google everything!) and know your resources. Know what's there before there's a crisis.

- Find someone who has experience in dealing with the issues of aging parents, just like you would if you were having problems with your car. Recognize that there are friends, organizations, and professionals who can help.

- Your friends who have been through the experience with aging parents will be another great resource – ask them for advice. What approaches and what services worked for them?

- Online research is helpful and massive. Yet, often word of mouth is the best way to discover effective resources. Talk to health care professionals, professionals in gerontology, other people in the same situation, their extended families and to your parents' doctor.

- The more you 'network' the more you find out – and it just requires research, research, and more research! The time you spend will definitely pay off for your parents and for you!

- Start your research now by going to the Epilogue of this book where I have listed some key websites, organizations, and readable, helpful books.

About Support

- Dealing with the issues of aging is not just natural and not everyone knows what to do, so it is OK to seek out help.

- Talk about your situation and get support. Don't deal with things in isolation, but intentionally build a support network.

- Find people who do not judge or give advice, but who are willing to just listen.

- Take the time to find a support group that is a good fit for you – it could be through church, through a local senior organization that has caregiver support groups, or a good group of friends.

- Use this time to build and strengthen relationships with your parents and siblings. Bring your children into the support circle and find ways that they can help their grand-parents and help you.

About Communication

- Listen to your parents – to what they are *really* saying. That isn't the natural thing to do in a family – everyone is going at a faster pace. Slow down, listen, communicate.

- Pay attention to the signals or cues that things with your parents are changing – when there is an inability to do something that a parent could always do (remember those 'defining moments?').

- Laugh every day.

- In all that you say and do, have patience, patience, patience. Slow down and be with your parents in the moment.

About Matters of the Heart

- Understand the changes in your parents' mood and what your parents are feeling.

- Be quicker to forgive than to judge.

- Don't hold on to negative things from the past – let go of bad memories.

- Make peace with your parents if you do not already have it.

- Be kind and tolerant.

- Be easy on yourself and let go of guilt as you struggle to meet your parents' needs.

- You cannot take things personally – your parents are not doing anything to you. It is so much worse for them, what is happening to them.

- Encourage your parents and they will show appreciation.

- Give the best care that you can so that you can look in the mirror and know that you did it right and finished well.

- Even in difficult times, it is an honor to take care of aging parents. Be grateful for their long lives.

- Be at peace with the decisions that you ultimately make.

- Forgive your parents for their weaknesses – and celebrate their strengths! Do the same for yourself.

Optimism and Positive Approaches

Just as the common thread of dedication emerges as the key ingredient for the adult children who were interviewed, there is a strong common thread woven throughout their recommendations – the common thread of optimism – focusing on the positive and hopeful. Clearly, optimism doesn't come easily. Sometimes, it is not even desirable. Feelings of anger, anxiety, resentment all need to be expressed at times. That's where the support system comes into play!

My friend, Joann, who I earlier identified as a recipient of my imagined "Daughter of the Year" award for the absolute dedication she has to a quite difficult mother, recognizes this need as she emails the following to me:

"All the books I have and all the new ones on the bookshelves about children with their aging parents always show loving elderly people smiling with their beautiful children smiling about coping – how about the truth? My hands around my mother's throat with my eyes bulging out while she's smiling pulling cookies out of her pocket that I hid because she's diabetic, and due to her dementia, she forgot that she just ate!" We laughed as we later on discussed the possibility of this image portrayed on the cover of this book!

Joann knows that she can express this kind of frustration to me – I am part of her support system and I have been through the experience of dementia with my own mother. She knows that I am a "safe place." She also knows that I know how important it is to say the negative so that you can focus on the positive. She also shares, *"There have been wonderful moments that I will always remember – today, when I was putting on my makeup she asked if I would put some on her, and after I did, she took my hand and said she's so happy to be in my home."*

Closing Thoughts – Two Meanings of Hope

So, how is it possible to follow the recommendations cited here that speak to optimism, to positive approaches, to hope? I would like to offer one possibility – and that is a new way of thinking about hope. Hear me out.

When I was studying ethics at The Center for Healthcare Ethics in Orange, California, specifically related to aging and end-of-life issues, I was presented with a concept that talked about "Hope #1" and "Hope #2." Hope #1 is the "Cure Hope" that says, "I believe that my loved one will get well." This is the hope that we embrace when someone, young or old, has a sudden illness or setback, and the prognosis is for complete, or at least, significant recovery.

Hope #1 is also the hope that we carry when there are subtle changes in our parents' abilities and together, with them, we can find resources and strategies to maintain their independence. It is good hope. It is appropriate hope – until the time that it becomes true that things are not going to get better. If we cling to Hope #1 when it is no longer useful, when things are not going to get better, then it is almost inevitable that we will become angry, resentful or frustrated. We are hoping for something that cannot come true.

Hope #2 is the "All-Embracing Hope" that says, "I believe that there is meaning no matter how things turn out." It is this larger meaning of hope that allows us, even when faced with a parent's irreversible decline, physically and/or mentally, to focus on the positive over the negative, to be optimistic rather than pessimistic, and to have hope rather than despair. It is the hope that opens opportunities for building deep relationships in the most trying of times. It is the hope that overcomes communication barriers and allows us to listen and really hear. It is the hope that transcends pain and suffering, and brings our parents and ourselves to a place of acceptance and peace.

There is meaning, no matter how things turn out.

ACT II

About Our Own Aging

— ❤️ —

As Told by
Voices of Hope

Introduction to Act II

Peace About Parent Care

*T*he passing of time certainly creates strong and significant challenges for our aging parents. We, the adult children, have a multitude of responsibilities and opportunities to encircle them with love and support. We have learned from our Cast, the *Voices of Experience*, that caring for aging parents, can be difficult, frustrating and ultimately, sad. Yet, this caregiving can also deeply enrich our lives and form stronger bonds across the family. This is all the natural timing of life, the natural progression of life events. Most of us are able to arrive at a place of peace as we face the decline and death of our parents.

Unsettling Issues for the Mid-Life "Kids"

However, as we journey through parent care, we start to form new thoughts and questions about ourselves. What are those thoughts about the passing of time that keep gently nagging at us and create an unsettling feeling? Concerns about our own health issues begin to creep into conversations with our friends. *You know this is true!* It may be time to sign up for Medicare. A pension check may have replaced our paycheck. We sometimes long for the past and think of it as an easier, happier time. Or we simply can't believe how much time has passed, that more of our life is behind us than in front of us. Questions and fears about mortality surface. It may be that as we care for our parents in their final years, days, moments of their lives, we analyze this journey of time and realize that we, too, are not so young anymore.

This brings us to the question that many of us have begun to ask, *When did we get this old?* We may ask this question with a hint of humor, but likely there is a serious component to the question as well.

We may be young at heart; we may think that we fit the description of the current cliché of 60 being the new 40; we may be planning for a second or a third career. This is all great! But the truth is, that in addition to the many positive aspects of our lives, a huge hunk of our lives is in the past, our parents may no longer be with us, and if we haven't had plastic surgery and/or cosmetic "procedures", we may not look quite how we would like to.

Now is the time for those of us in mid-life to enthusiastically but realistically face our own future and carefully craft what we want it to be. We want to do this in the same way that enlightened our perspective of caring for our parents – with joy, laughter, gratitude and hope. As our Cast grapples with the issues of their own aging and become the *Voices of Hope,* we will discover how to put these four great qualities into practice for our own lives.

9

Our Parents, Ourselves

"I look at my parents and try to continue what I like and discontinue what I don't like."

~Terry

When we were teenagers and possibly into young adulthood, most of us probably made the remark at some time or another, *"When I grow up, I definitely won't be like my parents!"* Our parents, we thought, were too strict, too closed-minded, too old-fashioned, or just plain too old. Of course, to feel this way is normal. It's our job as teenagers to strive desperately to become individuals. And, of course, we had some very cool friends who understood our needs, wants, and desires far better than our parents ever could. A few of these friends are still close friends; others, we can't even remember their names.

By young adulthood, most of us have made a transition and established ourselves, mentally and emotionally, in a way that is independent from our parents. Often, at the same time, though, we develop a slowly growing appreciation for our parents and our upbringing.

I'm not sure exactly when the next transition in the adult child-parent relationship happens. Sometime in early mid-life, probably as we are raising our own children or thinking about our next career step, we recognize, and sometimes are amazed, that, to some degree, we begin to think many of the same things that our parents thought. We start saying many of the same things that they said. In fact, we act in the exact way we always swore we never would! We are essentially developing an active approach to life that incorporates important pieces of what our parents once taught us.

Of course, this may not be true if the parent-child relationship was always negative or possibly abusive. In those situations, the adult child's life philosophy will hopefully be based on the opposite of what was modeled.

But for our discussion here, let's continue to listen to the positive outlook of our Cast, now our *Voices of Hope*, who have dedicated so much of their time to caring for aging parents. It is remarkable to listen to how the perceived realities of their parents' lives and their role as caregivers have shaped and strengthened some very lovely and long-lasting philosophies about life on this earth. They are philosophies that are serving these particular mid-life adults well as they travel along their own journey of life. If you listen to them carefully, you may be able to construct your own life philosophy, even if you are in the midst of difficult circumstances, which will lead you to a more fulfilling life.

Toward a Balanced, Enriched Philosophy of Life

Depth and Direction

As we move into mid-life, we can be so busy with our work, our children, our homes and our multitude of activities that we don't stop to think where all of this is taking us. We plan every minute of our day and then fall into bed exhausted at night. Although the demands of taking care of an aging parent can add to our "to-do" list, the very essence of providing that care may also cause us to slow down our thinking process and start to prioritize what is really important. We begin to ponder more deeply and more intentionally about what matters.

When asked how taking care of her mother contributed to her current philosophy of life, Patsy reflects that, *"Every day is a gift, so I want to do well by others and by God."* For her, *"life is a journey – sometimes you get to take the lead, and sometimes life takes the lead. Life is about finding a balance – how much time to spend with aging parents, with your kids, at work . . ."*

The years that Patsy spent involved with caring for her mother added both depth and direction to how she thinks about life and how she lives her life. In terms of living her life, she plans for her senior years and retirement in a very intentional way. She learned from her mother about the importance of financial planning and living trusts. *"I now know the importance of planning to be financially sound and also having a good life."* Her mother had planned well which allowed the family to seek out care and resources without financial worries.

Patsy also learned from her mother's experience *"that it is not so bad as a senior single woman."* You may recall that Patsy's mother developed a whole second life as a real estate agent after her husband died. *"I've learned that becoming older isn't always so scary. I can handle it."*

Through taking care of her mother, Patsy became more grounded in a *"joy of life"* perspective. The caregiving experience underscored the importance of making a contribution to the world. *"It is important to have the time to do things that make a difference. I put greater value on the time that I spend with my grandson. There is always a lot of opportunity as we go on with life and we can always find a way to make things work."*

Building on Love and Creativity

There are some very fortunate families that thrive on the ability to encourage each other in ways that are individual, creative and supportive. Although many of us are nurtured in a reasonably positive environment, some families stand out as extraordinary in their capacity for building strength and courage. Parents who promote an atmosphere of freedom and acceptance will likely reap the benefits with children who are brave and feel free to give and to love.

Prior to her caregiving experience, Ellis already enjoyed a creative and freeing philosophy of life that she attributes almost exclusively to her parents. She states that, *"in life, you must have a few really deep friendships (which may be members of your family) in which you can totally be yourself, and those friends accept you for all of your faults and all of your gifts."* She chose gerontology as a profession *"because it allows me to be vulnerable. I don't have to be perfect and can let my weaknesses show. Older people accept you for who you are – you don't have to be anyone but who you are."*

Through her dedication to providing care to her aging parents, she now *"loves life even more. I have a special love for elderly people, and now through my own parents, that love has grown stronger."*

Although Ellis focuses on the positive in life, her experience with her parents has made her *"more aware of life's markers – birth, baptism, marriage, death – I am more cognizant now of the losses, but try not to focus on them."* Even as she copes with the sadness of her parents' decline—she grieves over her mother's recent death, and sometimes struggles with patience in her interactions with her father —her deepening passion for life has strengthened her belief *"that you need to do something in life that makes a difference in the lives of others. We are here to help each other through this journey. This entails some Christian values such as forgiveness, and 'do unto others' . . . It also entails some Zen-like qualities, such as getting rid of the ego. Remaining humble, sensitive, compassionate – these are great qualities to strive for."*

A New Understanding

Even if not extraordinary, many of us can say that our family upbringings were above average. We had reasonable expectations of how our life would evolve. We strive to be positive, but sometimes find ourselves in a downward spiral with worries about our parents, our children and ourselves. Yet, through the caregiving experience that involves our inner selves so deeply and richly, we begin to find a new philosophy that reaches in a new direction with a new understanding.

Dawn had a rather dramatic change in her life philosophy as a result of her aging parent journey. *"Life is the pits and anything good is a bonus"* was the approach that she adopted in her earlier years to get through her day-to-day life. The years that she spent, as an only child, nurturing, helping, holding her aging parents – helped her come to a new understanding of life. Now she says, *"Life is peaks and valleys. When you are in a valley, a peak is just around the corner. Attitude is everything when living through difficult times, but often the worst fears don't materialize. You always have to hang on to the hope."*

Overcoming Adversity

Sometimes this new understanding does not evolve gently as it did for Dawn. There was a more dramatic "philosophy of life" change for Peter whose parents had been very difficult through-out his life. As a result of the caregiving process and then the death of both parents, Peter emerged with a fresh and positive outlook about how to live his own life.

Peter is the youngest of those that I interviewed, on the ear-lier side of mid-life. He says that, *"I was a pretty selfish person. The way I was raised, I was the baby—my mom did everything for me. Then when my mom needed so much care and attention, I saw how my wife was willing to be of service and sacrifice her own needs to help my mother. Then I knew that it was time to give back, and I want to be the best that I can be so that I can serve others and be more sacrificial. When I am giving or loving, I get so much in return. I am kind of in the 'on-deck' circle– my mom and dad are dead – there is a time when you want to start giving back."*

There certainly could have been a completely different philosophical outcome for Peter. He shared many times during his interview that his mother embodied the dichotomy of doing everything for him while also being emotionally abusive and distant during his childhood and into adulthood. She was difficult and demanding. Peter struggled to overcome his emotional damage and provide care and support to her. Many people in this situation would become bitter, resentful and take on a selfish perspective that focuses on taking care of "me." That would not only be understandable, but maybe even helpful for a time. The problem becomes that bitterness and resentment are heavy baggage to carry around and can become crippling to self-care as well as to service to others. This heavy load can break our spirit.

So how did Peter manage to emerge from his tumultuous caregiving experience with a philosophy of wanting to give back, wanting to serve others? The first reason is that which he states above – the example that his wife set with her willingness to sacrifice her own needs to help with the care of his mother, her mother-in-law.

The second reason he stated is that he renewed and strengthened his relationship with God as he faced taking care of parents with whom he had not been emotionally or spiritually close. In sharing about his faith, he says that the foundation of how he views life now is, *"to know, love and serve God. I have learned that life is so temporal, and what we have is ultimately not ours."*

Continuation of Values

There are also families who are rock solid in their values, ethics and beliefs. And to the credit of the oldest generation, somehow these attributes are passed down through the generations without tumult or doubts or lasting rebellion. The caregiving experience serves to reinforce this strong foundation. The foundation may be built on some form of religious ground, a humanitarian approach, or a simple belief in the goodness of people.

Kathi's ideas about life have always come from the Christian philosophy introduced by her mom and dad. Her parents introduced her to this way of believing by going to church and taking her to Sunday school. *"There was a point in about the sixth grade,"* she says, *"when I realized the importance of the Bible – that it is the main document that I should live by. My parents were integral in this."*

When asked if providing care to her parents, particularly with the suffering that her father has endured over many years, has changed her philosophy in any way, she replied, *"This has just validated my philosophy in a new way – that God is working in everything. God is working in all things, though they don't necessarily come out good. I try to think that God is working in this toward ultimate good and ultimate reconciliation. It's a new paragraph in a chapter."* As she speaks, it is clear that the beliefs that she first learned from her parents provide her with a true sense of purpose as she shares her time and gives of herself to provide them with a more enriched life.

I need to interject again, as I did with Peter's story, that a negative outlook could surely have been the result in Kathi's situation.

Anger at God seems like a more human reaction to the long-term suffering of her very devout dad. That was my reaction when my dad died. My dad who was a pastor and bishop; my dad who only got to enjoy four years of retirement after a lifetime of serving God; my dad who lost his gift of speech because of the poison of radiation. Yes, I was very angry and questioned the very existence of a higher power that would allow my dad to die in this way.

Kathi is lucky. She holds a form of faith that transcends the expectation that God will make sure that only good things will happen to good people. She is able to believe in what she calls *"an ultimate good"* that is not based just on what happens on this earth. I wish I were that lucky.

Mike's parents were also the source of his outlook on life from the beginning until now. He lives by: *"Enjoy every moment. Give something back. Appreciate your family and friends always."* He continues, *"This philosophy directly and fully emanated from my parents. This has always been my philosophy."* This is remarkable because Mike shared previously how he had been a problem child, a "horrible" son. Yet, through those probably rather typical years for which Mike says he has *"regrets about past behavior,"* the life lessons that his father modeled as a doctor and his mother nurtured as a homemaker were his foundation for the years to come. *"My father dealt with life and death, so he knew how precious life was, and how quickly it could end."* Our parents, ourselves.

A Practical, Purpose-Filled Philosophy

At the end of the day, many of us will look to a very practical philosophy. We will have learned from our parents, especially from the caregiving experience whenever that occurs. We have persevered, done our best, and ultimately we take a deep breath and wonder what all of this means. How do we live our own lives? What do we do the same as our parents? What should we do differently?

Terry, our directly honest pragmatist, discusses his philosophy of life, which does reflect his experience as an adult son. He says, *"Live and let live – it's OK that people live differently than me. I have developed much of my philosophy from my dad – he has always been accepting. I know now that there are lots of ways to do things – not just my way. I don't try to change other people."*

With the aging and increasing frailty of his parents, Terry says that he does think about life a bit differently. *"I used to think that 'all is well that ends well' – but now I know that there is a lot of process along the way that is important. It is not just the end that matters. As we grow older, enjoying the smaller things along the way is more important than looking forward to the next event."*

Terry is honest, and again pragmatic, as he shares how his parents have affected his way of thinking. ***"I look at my parents and try to continue what I like and discontinue what I don't like."*** This statement should apply to most of us. *It is possibly the most important idea about crafting a philosophy of life.* Even if the core of our philosophy and beliefs has come from our parents, there are pieces of their lives that simply don't fit into ours. We look for that blend of what they have taught us and what we have learned through our own experiences to create a way of thinking, a philosophy of life that brings us close to a full measure of contentment and gratitude.

Terry gives a specific example of a *"discontinued"* way of thinking. *"My mom has never been satisfied if not everyone in the family can get together. When we are all together, she'll say, 'why do you have to leave so soon? When can we get together again?' I am trying to change my response to a positive one – 'Wasn't it great that we could get together?' I try to do this with my own kids. Why make people feel badly when they have come to visit you?"*

I worked in a retirement community for many years. I counseled with residents; I counseled with their families – and it was always very clear to me how the attitude of the older parents affected the adult children. When the parents accepted change, focused on their strengths, and had realistic expectations of the people in their lives, families were close and there was a shared philosophy of how life could still be fulfilling – even in a retirement home, even at an advanced age. When parents were of the nature to complain and were bitter about their circumstances – guess what? – the adult children complained and were bitter as well. You could call that a "shared philosophy" but I don't think you could find much to carry forward as a mid-life adult to enhance a meaningful life. Only resentment and regrets.

Closing Thoughts About Philosophy

So our first glance at mid-life adulthood sees the importance of integrating a philosophy into our daily lives that allows us to accept where we are in time and move into the future with a positive, yet discerning outlook. We can take the best of what we have learned from our parents. That may be as practical as financial planning, as affirming as an appreciation for family and friends, as politically correct as accepting other ways of life, as transcendental as a strong faith in a higher power, or as simplistic as making the most of each day because time is passing.

We can discard what we could clearly see did not work well for them - those characteristics that can cause aging parents to be the biggest obstacle to their own care: Pride, impatience, unwillingness to make changes, rejecting resources, unrealistic expectations. Or, as Terry stated, we can *"discontinue"* patterns that we don't like. And then we can add more sustaining qualities that we have discovered partially from our parents through the caregiving experience, and maybe sometimes just because of our own mid-life reflections. These might include compassion, humility, sensitivity, service to others, empathy . . . you can add your own here.

Key Learning Points

- As an outcome of parent caregiving, mid-life adults can begin to create a philosophy about their own older years.

- With discerning observation, adult children can reject those qualities that have not served their parents well, embrace those that have worked, and adopt new characteristics that may enhance their own aging experience.

- The balance is dependent on taking the best of what has helped aging parents and adding our personal perspective to move forward in time with grace, optimism, and hope.

Time for Writing and Reflection

1. If your parents are living, ask them and write about what qualities they think have allowed them to age the most successfully and how those have translated into positive living in their older years. Ask them if there are any characteristics that they would change if they could go back in time and have a "do-over."

2. Write down, in simple terms, what your philosophy of life is. Have your parents influenced this philosophy? If so, in what way?

3. Brainstorm about what characteristics you would like to carry forward in your life philosophy as you age. Describe what characteristics you have observed in your parents that you want to discontinue. Write about how the characteristics that you keep and those you discard will influence your behavior and your quality of life.

IO

The Middle Years:
The Good and the Not-So-Good

"I have gotten broader in my interests ... I feel like I am on the cusp of doing something completely different ..."

~Kathi

Mid-life is a complex mixture of some great opportunities and insights blended with some really tough stuff that can bring us down. I am not going to underplay the tough stuff. It is real. I am experiencing it. However, I am also going to share with you what our Cast has shared as vibrant and hopeful aspects of mid-life that can be cause for celebration. Since most of us like to hear the good news first, we will start our discussion on how the passing years can give us new and positive perspectives on life. The not-so-good news – the tough stuff - clearly needs to be acknowledged and explored. So we will also look at the problematic issues of mid-life through the eyes of our Cast and see if we can discover ways to accept and overcome them.

To prepare notes for this chapter, I studied my interviews multiple times. Then, I made a side-by-side list of the good and the not-so-good aspects of mid-life that were shared. I have to admit that I was a bit anxious about doing this. What if the "bad list" was longer than the "good list"? What would I share with you, the reader? Let's find out.

The Good

The first piece of good news is that, according to our Cast, there are more good than bad issues associated with mid-life. So the "good" outweighs the "bad." Not bad, right? Let's explore these good aspects, one by one. I believe that you will recognize many of them.

Gratitude

At the top of the good list, there was an unexpected, but strongly felt affirmation of mid-life —the bold recognition that our time here is at least half over, maybe more. Why is this on the top of the good side, you ask? Because if we are willing to recognize where we are in time, and not live with the delusion that we are going to live forever, we can live our lives better than we did in the past. As Peter says, *"My life is half over and I don't want to live it the way that I have. I want to be more loving and caring to my family and to myself. I no longer take things for granted . . . I want to be less selfish."*

This bold recognition will allow us to live out our lives in a new way, grateful for the years that we still have. And we can be grateful that we have an enlightened vision of how to play the new roles that we take on – now and in future years.

Gratitude is a critical component for living with purpose in mid-life. It is so important that I have dedicated an entire chapter, Chapter 13, to exploring more thoroughly the positive impact on our lives when we are grateful.

Your Second, Third or Maybe Fourth Act

Many of our mid-life voices spoke about having more discretionary time and an increased flexibility with how they could now manage that time. If we can gather up the courage to do something new, this is one of the absolute greatest gifts mid-life can give. Something we have always wanted to do. Something we just thought of for the first time but that now sounds exciting with our newfound perspective. Maybe something totally out of character!

The late Frank McCourt won the Pulitzer Prize for his first published book, *Angela's Ashes,* at age 66. In an article that he wrote for *The Los Angeles Times* (*Parade* Magazine, March, 2008) he shares that he had been a teacher for 30 years when he had an "epiphany." McCourt says in his article that he realized, "I didn't want to talk anymore. I wanted to go home and make little marks on paper." Those little marks turned into a best-selling novel, and he wrote several more books after that. He also tells us that the famous novelist F. Scott Fitzgerald wrote, "There are no second acts in American lives." McCourt challenges that statement and claims that "We all can have second acts (and third!)." He adds, "Don't settle for less: find what you love and do it." Fitzgerald died at age 44, so for him, his own words were probably true.

But we, today, can adopt the same way of thinking as Mc-Court. Many of us will live into our seventies, eighties, nineties, and possibly beyond, with reasonably good physical and mental health. If we are brave, we can have Second, Third, Fourth Acts in our lives. We can avoid that obsessive feeling of regret if we simply try new things. The result may not be a Pulitzer Prize, but it may be the best prize of your lifetime – a blue ribbon for being truly proud of yourself! At the end of the *Parade* magazine article, McCourt shares, "Along the way, I'm learning to play the guitar. Act Four, coming up."

Experience and Enrichment

Since I first interviewed Patsy for this book, she has transitioned into a rewarding Second Act. After nearly 20 years as a department head for a major metropolitan city, working an average of 55 to 60 hours a week year-round, she now teaches part-time at a local university. Patsy's working hours have decreased to about 25 a week with time off during the holidays and all through the summer. It used to be difficult for her to take just one week of vacation. However, a lighter workload is just one small part of the value of her new position.

She was ready to make a change, to get away from City Council meetings, Commission meetings, community task forces, weekend city events. She loved her job and was highly respected throughout her community, but she was growing somewhat weary of the pressure and the politics. Equipped with her Master of Social Work (MSW) degree she says, *"I'm using my* education, skills and experience in a different setting, a different role, and a different way . . . a new way that is challenging, interesting and rewarding, both personally and professionally."

Patsy is teaching graduate students who are working toward their MSW. About her students, she states, *"Working directly with a diverse group of motivated adults is stimulating and forces me to stay current . . . The quality and commitment of these graduate students to address tough issues gives me hope for the future of our country and our world."*

However, there is an important question to be asked. How does Patsy feel about descending on the organizational chart from the top as a department head to somewhere in the middle as a part-time college faculty member? *"Mostly I find it liberating,"* she says, *"to be able to focus on the students and how I can contribute to their learning experience versus hours upon hours of administrative meetings, re-writing contracts or policies, and dealing with multi-million-dollar budget challenges and personnel issues. Now working 25 hours a week to teach three classes seems a good balance for me . . . this schedule gives me structure and purpose to my time."*

A downside to her new university career is that *"the pay is dramatically less, although it does help support opportunities to travel and other interests."* This is more than offset for Patsy by the upside that, *"there seems to be some prestige to being a 'college professor' . . . but for me, much of the motivation is giving back and building a better world by helping develop a strong cadre of social work leaders."*

For Patsy, then, she strives to balance the "downsizing" of her status and salary with the "upsizing" of making a direct contribution to the students in her care. Although she had to make some personal and financial adjustments, the outcome for Patsy has proven both rich and satisfying. I recently had breakfast with her, and she expressed how gratifying her Second Act is to her. She saved and planned wisely during her hectic administrative years and now is fully enjoying the impact she has on a new generation of social workers.

A Return to Past Interests

Our Cast member Kathi was a voice major in college and went on to work for the Los Angeles Opera. Although she is not one of their performers, she has worked in the classical music environment for most of her professional life. She loves music; she loves opera. But, she has not only loved music throughout her 60-plus years of life, she has also loved animals. However, her full-time, demanding schedule didn't allow her to stay active in humane issues related to animals or to spend time in her love of horseback riding.

In recent years, Kathi has become more and more aware of some of the abhorrent treatment of animals in our country, and she has become active in supporting legislation to protect animals. She has also become very personally involved and now has several horses that she has saved from slaughter. In addition, Kathi often fosters cats until they can be placed in a good home.

As Kathi approached retirement from the opera, which had been a very satisfying career, she dreamt of "new arenas of activity." She says, ***"I have gotten broader in my interests*** – *it* was opera for so long – now, and maybe it's a part of the wisdom, there is a different kind of confidence . . . **I feel like I am on the cusp of doing something completely different**, *probably related to animals."* Kathi now spends time researching the animal rescue movement, and she is well on her way to significant involvement in the horse rescue efforts – a very courageous and much-needed Second Act! A Second Act whose opening curtain caught her by surprise.

Courage and Creativity

You are now reading my Second Act – or actually, it could probably be classified as my Third Act. I have had a long career in gerontology/geriatric long-term care which included social services, administration, and teaching healthcare and end-of-life ethics. Interwoven into that career was the raising of three children – so I kind of had an Act One and an Act Two playing out at the same time, sometimes in chaotic fashion, sometimes in harmony.

About 10 years ago, I started saying what so many people say in conversation, "I should write a book about this." My *"this"* was the beauty and the agony, the joy and the sorrow, the laughter and the tears that co-exist as people get older. I heard stories of these competing feelings over and over from my very old residents and/ or their fairly old adult children. My *"epiphany"* was that it is vital to share, to commiserate, to laugh and to cry about all that happens with the passing of time. I decided to try to write that down, as scared as I am to put my thoughts out into the world. But I'm moving forward with courage because of the rich and important information that so many people have shared with me. In my Third Act, I am making these little marks on my computer. And I will finish it, and I will have no regrets. I will share, in whatever way possible, all that I have learned from those who have shared with me with the hope of making your life a little bit better.

I found a fascinating article in *Aging Today,* published by The American Society on Aging, called, "Older Workers Can Reap New Rewards by Climbing the Corporate . . . Lattice?" by Jeff Schwartz (*Aging Today,* November – December 2012). The article speaks to an even broader concept of how older people will find meaning and meet challenges throughout their life span. Schwartz builds on the idea put forth by his colleagues, Cathleen Benko and Molly Anderson, in their book *The Corporate Lattice: Achieving High Performance in the Changing World of Work.* He shares their concept that in the 21st century, people are navigating their careers away from a linear ascent up the corporate ladder to a lattice model in which careers move up, down, and side-to-side according to the needs and interests of the worker.

Schwartz says that, "It is time to extend this lattice perspective to our entire lives." His idea is that in the lattice career perspective of life, people develop a growing portfolio of skills and experiences enabling them to remain engaged in work, family and social life. He envisions a country in which older people return to school, equip themselves for new jobs, remain socially active — a distinctive shift from the "traditional once-and-done approach." The lattice approach moves older people away from bingo parlors and buffet lines . . . and "positions the escalating aging population to remain a vital cohort that contributes to all aspects of society."

This certainly broadens the notion of a Second or Third Act as an addition to our older years into an integrated philosophy of multiple acts all through life. I like this idea! And I have never liked bingo (plus I never win!).

Self-Acceptance

Each member of our mid-life Cast embraces a growing capacity for self-acceptance. We have all probably wasted way too much time in our younger years with self-doubt, self-criticism, and a variety of insecurities. We may still succumb to these negative self-judgments at times. But how nice to be at a stage in life when it is possible and within reach to openly applaud our strengths, recognize and forgive ourselves for our weaknesses, and mostly be at a place of peace from within.

Ellis expresses these thoughts well when she says, *"The most positive aspect of reaching the middle years of life is being comfortable with who I am – knowing my gifts and my limitations. When you're younger, you compare yourself to your peers. Now I am at a point of 'Who gives a damn?'"*

Similarly, Dawn says, *"I am now more at peace with who I am, more accepting of who I am. I was always hard on myself and now I can recognize what my strengths are."*

And Terry tells us how good it feels to *"be comfortable with yourself and recognize that your place in the world is very positive"* – to which he adds – *"I'm not going to be the President and I really don't give a shit."* Self-acceptance is a powerful tool to carry in your pocket as you confront the challenges of mid-life.

The Wisdom Thing

A companion to self-acceptance can be the recognition that experience, maturity and the wisdom of years are qualities to cherish. This is not to say that in mid-life we have achieved perfection in acquiring these qualities, but we are a lot closer to attaining them than 10, 20 or 30 years ago. And these qualities do command respect from all age groups.

Kathi says, *"I perceive that people listen to me more – there is more of a respect. I also expect that from people – I expect them to listen to me because there is a validity to what I say. I have experienced it. It's not just ideas. Others recognize that I have the years of wisdom."*

Patsy chooses *"experience in both life and work"* as the most positive aspect of being in mid-life. She knows the resources that she can draw on for her personal life and for her financial stability. In addition, this experience, this knowledge of resources, expands her awareness and confidence, leading to a fuller, more interesting life of *"freedom and flexibility."*

And Mike? He says it most simply and directly – his experience of years lived gives him the wisdom *"not to sweat the small stuff."*

Self-acceptance can also engender the ability to actively affirm and encourage others, whether it is your aging parents, spouse, children, colleagues or friends. Doesn't it feel so uplifting for your own self when you can honestly praise another? This comes from wisdom.

Ellis says, *"I have learned over the years that the secret to life is everyone needs to be encouraged. You need to tell people they are doing a good job. You need to encourage your husband, your children – and say, 'I am so proud of you!' Show your admiration!"* In mid-life, we can freely show our admiration – we *must* freely show our admiration! We have little to lose, and much to gain, especially in terms of our many and diverse relationships.

If you have a difficult time complimenting others, just give it a try, even if it is forced. I predict that you will feel internally rewarded. And you will have made the day for someone else.

Quality of Relationships

Deeper relationships often accompany the passing of years. Our Cast tells us that in a subtle way we start to realize that our time is limited. Combined with this recognition is the understanding that our connection with others is at the very core of our well-being. We seek stronger and intentionally honest professional relationships. We build more intimate personal relationships.

Dawn says that because she can now recognize what her strengths are, she is very successful in relating to other people. *"I am successful in the business world because I can build relationships,"* she notes.

Ellis has also found that her work relationships have taken on a new depth. *"Women at a young age are especially competitive. Now my relationships with women are deep and sensitive. After I reached my forties, my relationships with women became so rich. I don't have to worry about competition and have found mentoring relationships with other women in both my work and my personal life."*

Ellis also expresses that *"the relationship with my husband changes and deepens, and also becomes more mellow as we both mature."*

Relationships with children may evolve into mutually satisfying interactions, with more "give and take" and a fuller understanding of the other person's needs. Patsy identifies the changing nature of her relationship with her children as one of the most positive aspects of reaching the middle years of life. She says, *"There is the joy of having children who are now older and knowing that they are good people. It is a relief to focus on them as people, not just as my children."*

Taking self-doubt, competition, immaturity and fear out of our interactions will lead to much stronger and truer ties with people at work, in our communities, and at home.

An Open Mind

Following this same thread of improving with "age" – no, I'm not going to give the wine example – can be the ability to be more open to differences. Our Cast tells us to throw away those immature, judgmental natures! This is probably a work-in-progress for most of us. I think it is safe to say, though, that a person can accept differences far more easily when self-acceptance is a stronger presence than in earlier years.

Terry says that *"being able to accept differences"* is the most important factor of being in mid-life for him. For him, an open mind toward others is especially important. He originally comes from a small town with a very homogenous population. He realized at an early age that there was a stark lack of acceptance of differences.

I am going to even go a bit further here to say that by mid-life, we are more likely to accept the differences in our own children, who are now probably young adults. When they are little, cute and primarily under our control, it's easy, and probably normal, to envision them as extensions of ourselves. We imagine their academic achievements, successful careers and happy marriages. Of course, we hope that when they become adults, they will live close to us and be a part of our daily lives.

As we move toward our fifties or sixties, it is far more probable that we have the capacity to realize that our children must follow their own path. They need to make their own mistakes, learn from their own experiences, and evolve into separate and probably very different people from ourselves. This may also still be a work-in-progress. Terry admits that, *"It's difficult accepting the limited control of parenthood."* I agree. I have to challenge myself every day to accept that all three of my young-adult children are choosing a path that is separate from me in their walk of life.

As mid-life adults, there is much to embrace. We can embark on new adventures to create second, third and fourth acts that enrich the lives of others and ourselves. We can be content with who we are, accepting our strengths and our weaknesses. We can more deeply cherish our relationships, open our minds and accept a new and different world, and be grateful for what we currently have and for the new opportunities that each day provides.

The Not-so-Good

OK – now is the time to turn to the "not-so-good." There does have to be a downside to not being as young as we once were. As I sit here for hours writing this chapter, my right hip wants me to get up and move around. I don't think this would have been the case in years past.

I am not a believer in 60 being the new 40 with its corollary – let's ignore and deny anything difficult associated with aging. I am 65 years old. I may have more style than my mother did at my age—although I'm pretty sure that she thought she was stylish. And she was! It was a different time. I may have a slightly longer life expectancy due to constantly evolving medical procedures. I am probably more physically fit than my parents were, since I adhere to the increasing emphasis on exercise (although not all of my cohort does). And, since my husband and I have more informational resources to plan well financially, we may have more opportunities in retirement than my parents did.

But the fact remains that I am definitely not 40 – I don't look 40 and I don't feel 40. I think about things that I didn't think about when I was 40. In concert with this reality, two big "not-so-good" issues emerged about mid-life from the interviews. I will talk about one of those now, take a pause with some lesser issues, and save the other big issue for the end of the chapter.

Big Issue #1 – Health Concerns

As we grow older and hit our late forties and beyond, there are rising fears about health problems – fears that, when we were younger, never crossed our minds. And we do have some cause for concern in mid-life and beyond. Current research tells us that our baby boomer generation will live longer, but we are not living healthier. We are more likely to have high blood pressure, high cholesterol and diabetes than the previous generation. In addition, our generation has a higher percentage of obesity. And even with the increased emphasis on exercise that I previously mentioned, our work lives often cause us to be sedentary with little time for physical activity. Sounds a bit like lifestyle choices, doesn't it? To our credit, though, we do smoke less so we have lower rates of emphysema and heart attacks. However, the new cliché that sitting is the new smoking does ring true!

Mike says that he does have a *"fear about serious health problems. The reason that I have fear is that I don't want to be a burden to my wife and children. I don't want them to go through what I did with my parents. My parents had serious quality of life issues."*

When Dawn thinks about all of the years that she cared for her parents, she wonders *"what losses and challenges"* she will face one day and *"how she will cope with significant losses."* Dawn has great faith in her children when it comes to her future health. During her parents' illnesses, she openly talked with both of her adult sons about end-of-life issues. She discussed her feelings about what she considers to be a worthy quality of life—and when it is time to let go. Like Mike, though, she doesn't want them to feel that her care is a burden. She shares, *"I say to my kids, whatever decisions they make someday on my behalf, they will be the right decisions."* She states this with firm confidence due to the depth of their conversations surrounding health, life and death. Family conversations that explore how a parent wants to close out this life are not easy to have. But the understanding that emerges can transform the fear of burden into the knowledge that providing care will be an honor.

Patsy first talks about health concerns in a more esoteric way. She says that being in mid-life and having lost her parents makes her have to deal with her own mortality. Then she gets more practical and says, *"I ask myself, how many ski years do my legs have left?"* And . . . she continues to test that question by skiing as often as possible.

Terry approaches health issues with some humor, saying, *"I have physical limitations now that I wasn't aware of five years ago. I used to say that I couldn't do some physical activity because I hadn't been doing it recently – now I know that there are limitations related to age!"*

Peter – who is still in his early fifties – says, very directly, that a difficult part of being in mid-life is *"the body falling apart."* He's having issues with irregular heartbeats and struggles to maintain a healthy routine of diet and exercise. But Peter fights back, goes to the gym on a regular basis, and calls on his faith to strengthen his resolve to be physically active and eat well.

Perhaps your parents had certain diseases starting relatively close to the age that you are now. That can certainly be a cause for concern about issues with your own health coming in the not-too-distant future. My family history brings both cancer and Alzheimer's at relatively early ages to the health table which is very disconcerting. Consequently, my vitamins and supplements include anti-oxidants, anti-inflammatories, and "brain health support." More importantly, though, is my awareness of these health issues, but not an obsession with them. That allows me to go into prevention mode to the extent possible and focus on healthy living through diet, exercise (both physical and mental), and regular physical exams.

I have to admit, however, that this is not easy for me. In fact, it's really hard—and I hate the cliché of "diet and exercise!" I love to eat, and until recently, I have not enjoyed exercising. Exercise was always a push for me, not a pull – and I could not stick with a regimen. What has turned this around is that I now intentionally equate exercise with internal health rather than external good looks. I don't focus on weight loss, which is always a frustration for me. Instead, when I am pounding away on the treadmill, I mentally picture all of the positive actions that are taking place inside of my body. That gives me the motivation to keep going. And now I actually feel that pull to go back if I haven't worked out for a few days. Amazing!

As for eating, I am unleashing my creativity. I have started to use a wide variety of spices and herbs in my cooking that I never even considered before. Before, I just didn't take the time. And I have discovered that these new tastes are just as delicious as buttery, creamy, cheesy sauces. Again, amazing!

In my interviews with my Cast of "Character", I found that health issues are probably the key worry of mid-life that almost everyone shares. We can be grateful that we live in a time of preventive healthcare. There is definitely easy access to a variety of health-supportive diets and forms of exercise that will help us in our quest for well-being in our older years. It is our absolute responsibility, each one of us, to take advantage of them.

Sometimes health issues will be more serious and require medical intervention. We can also be grateful that we live in a time when advanced medical and surgical resources for treatment of conditions are available. Peter, the youngest of our Cast, was so plagued by his irregular heartbeats that he took a risk and underwent a procedure that has only existed for the past few years. It was successful and he now no longer fears that he will just die suddenly. Of course, this all translates into the importance of regular, thorough physicals and compliance with recommended treatments and medications.

Some Not-so-Big Issues

There are other, lesser concerns, though still important ones, which can cause us to fret somewhat during these middle years. Our Cast identifies some of the intermittent worries that can rob us of peace of mind.

Appearance

A concern about declining health may translate into what may seem to be a more frivolous concern about our appearance. How we look can be a reflection of our physical health, and it definitely affects our mental health. But mostly, it is about our own self-image. Our appearance can make us feel great or it can make us feel pretty awful.

We all know that we are not at our best when we have a "bad hair day." I think, especially for women, it is difficult that our hair is turning gray, possibly causing what we may think is a "permanent bad hair day." And we also face wrinkles, loose skin, and that evolving saggy neck. Dawn says, *"We live in a youth-oriented society, and it's hard not to be vain."* But later in her interview, she realizes that *"I am glad to be over 60 – I have an excuse not to look perfect."* She is able to draw on the strength of self-acceptance. And Dawn, like many mid-life women, is grateful for the grand variety of natural looking hair dye!

Physical Changes

Or we might find our conversations revolving around the aches and pains that we get while exercising or just going about our daily life. Just watch the younger people at your table during these discussions – they are rolling their eyes! It is a time of life when some mild limitations rear their somewhat unpleasant heads – and we love to talk about them. Though often not life-threatening at this point, or even really life-diminishing, those limitations can be hard to accept. It takes a concerted effort to compensate for some physical limitations by doing such things as changing our routine to include exercises and activities that are a little easier on the joints. I do Pilates rather than free weights. Maybe you go for a brisk walk now instead of a run in order to save your knees. And it takes grace and gratitude to look in the mirror and see all that is still so beautiful! Not always so easy, but so important.

The Mirror Image

The recognition that our peers are looking older can sometimes cause us to gaze at them in disbelief. When you go to your class reunion, do you wonder who all of those "old people" are? Then we realize that our peers are a reflection of our own self. Patsy finds that *"it is difficult to realize how much older we [ourselves and our friends] have all gotten."* Then she adds, laughing, *"You have to deal with your spouse's aging, too – maybe he doesn't get out of bed as easily as he used to – and then you can't deny your own aging."*

Nostalgia

In addition, a gentle grieving process may sadden us at times. As we learned in the chapter on grief, even if our parents have died a while ago, we do still miss them – terribly. We miss sharing with them the good things that are happening now. Peter wishes that he could share new music that he creates. Mike wishes that he could share new and exciting accomplishments of his family. Patsy wishes that her son could know his grandparents.

We probably don't think these things every day, and they don't interfere with a productive life. But they are passing thoughts that can make us all too aware of the passing of time. I would love to have afternoon coffee with my mom again—I can still smell the coffee brewing. Or just one more time, have my six-year-old daughter (now 29) say, *"Mom, sleep with me until I fall asleep."* It may help when we long for the past to remember how fortunate we are to have these memories – memories to make us smile.

As we get older, time is increasingly the dichotomy of friend and foe. We are so grateful that time has been kind to us. Many of us in mid-life are living active lives and are using our time to develop new interests and pursuits. Yet, time is becoming more measured, somewhat limited. Kathi is in better health and better shape than ever before, leading a more active life than in the past. Still she says that *"I have started measuring my time a little bit. I have to think in terms of how old I will be when I do something different. You have to measure, limit – when you were young, you didn't have to think about time."* Wouldn't we all love to grab time, hold it in our hands, and slow it down a bit? But it just keeps moving along, seemingly faster as the years go by.

With all of these issues related to aging, big or small, it is extremely important to realize that we are not alone in our worries. And it really is OK to admit to them and talk about them. Often, as we share these worries and concerns with our friends, they diminish in importance. We can feel comforted and supported. Sometimes, we can even laugh, really laugh! And be so grateful for our friends who are getting older too!

Big Issue #2 – Resistance to Change

What did our Cast reveal as the second biggest issue of mid-life? Not being enthusiastic about change; seeing change in terms of loss, unwanted change, forced change. This can permeate our being and lead to some pretty sad days.

Ellis moved from her home of many years in Huntington Beach, CA, to the Pacific Northwest for a better work position for her husband. She says, *"Feeling older is not wanting to adapt to changes. I long for the days when the kids were little. I don't want the change. I don't want to move. I don't want to leave my home."*

Changes in our younger years – marriage, work promotions, having children, moving to new locations – all point in the direction of life-building, of excitement that we have reached these milestones. Dreams are coming true. Changes later on in life are sometimes very hard not to see as losses. Retirement, perhaps; children moving away; scaling down because you don't need the big house anymore. These are not always easy to celebrate.

As I first wrote this, I thought about my daughter Chelsea's decision to move to New York City, almost six years ago now. She had been living with us during the year following her college graduation, exploring her various options for her immediate future. She has always lived fairly close to home. She is a dancer and aspiring actor, so New York has inevitably been a lure for her. I am very excited that she is brave enough to move there and see what she can make happen. And good things are starting to happen.

But the truth? I am also heartbroken that she is not part of my daily life. This is despite knowing that it was time for her to move on and figure out how she wants to make a contribution to this world. And even though she visits often, when she leaves I shed oceans of tears, flooding my pillow. I wake up in the night and feel like there is an elephant sitting on my chest – I can't breathe. I am like my friend Ellis – I don't want the change – I am not enthusiastic about change.

It's essential that we deal with the feelings that may come with unwanted change. That elephant sitting on our chest can turn into Big Issue #1 – health problems. My approach is to share with my girlfriends when unwanted change overtakes. It always seems that when I am particularly low, a close friend is in an exceptionally good place and can really listen and advise. And invariably – vice versa. Or you may prefer exercise, journaling, going to counseling or meditation and prayer. In whatever manner you can, lift the heaviness and allow enthusiasm to slowly take its place. Don't hesitate. Try to make peace with the change. Embrace the change. Breathe freely.

Closing Thoughts on the Middle Years

The middle years – the good and the not-so-good.

As our Cast says, the good is really, really good! We are alive. Most of us are in pretty good health. We like ourselves. We like other people. Other people like us. We can draw on our courage and the strength that has brought us this far to take on new challenges. We may reach new goals that we couldn't even envision when we were young.

And the not-so-good is mostly manageable.

Yes, we may have some health issues – but we are smart enough to investigate and research remedies and adapt to slightly different ways of taking care of our bodies.

We may long for the past sometimes, and wish that we were young again. But we are smart enough to only lapse into this way of thinking for brief periods of time and then let it go. It's not going to happen. And we can treasure the memories that are a part of times past.

And we may hate change. I do. I always have – even when I was young – and I always will. But we have the experience and the intelligence to know that it is only through change that we grow. And it is only through growth that we reach our potential as human beings – for however many years that we have left to make our mark on this earth.

Key Learning Points

- Mid-life is a balancing act that requires a focus on the many benefits that we achieve as we age – freedom, gratitude, new adventures, a better acceptance of self and of others.

- There are difficulties in mid-life with health changes and other unwanted changes related to career and family life that need to be recognized and thoughtfully managed to the extent possible.

- As we move through our mid-life years, it is essential that we carry and share optimism, courage, flexibility and hope – leading us to a place of wisdom that will help us and our loved ones lead a life not based on the "not-so-good" but on the "good."

Time for Writing and Reflection

1. Make your own "side-by-side" list of the good and the not-so-good aspects of your own life.

2. Journal about how you can continue to strengthen and embellish the "good" aspects of your mid-life journey.

3. Brainstorm with your spouse, significant other, and/or friends about how you can cope with and learn from the "not-so-good" items that are on your list. Share. Cry. Laugh.

If you don't have others to share with, continue with your personal journaling to create reasonable solutions to the "not-so-good" items on your list. Dig deep.

II

When Did We Get This Old?!?
Our Conversation

"Whatever walk I will be walking, I want to make a
positive difference. I am not afraid."
~*Kathi*

On our intricate path of the mid-life journey, we are looking for answers, for inspiration, for guidance, and for support. When I studied the questions that I developed for the final part of the interview with our Cast, I began to imagine their responses as a part of a support group discussion. I could envision them sitting in a circle, sharing with me, but mostly with each other. Sharing about coping with aging, accepting our place on the aging journey, keeping a sense of humor, and most of all, feeling grateful for what we have. All of these themes in some way relate to the overall, rhetorical question, *When Did We Get This Old?!?*

From this support group perspective, I write this and the next two chapters. As you come to the conversation portions of the chapters, envision yourself sitting in a circle with our Cast that you have come to know quite well. Listen to their thoughts and ideas. Then think about what your input would be.

Perceptions of Aging

Across the board, the question, *When Did We Get This Old?!?*, engenders an immediate recognition of a universal understanding behind that question. There is a knowing smile and laughter that yes, we *are* asking this very question, whether we are 30 or 60 or 90. Of course, no one actually thinks of themselves as "old" – old is always at least 20 years older than we are. Many people in their eighties and nineties don't want to move into a retirement community because they don't want to be around all of those "old" people. Just recently, my 95-year-old mother-in-law got huffy when my daughter referred to her age group as elderly. She said, *"We don't think of ourselves as elderly."* Well, when do you?

The truth is that this question, *When did we get this old?*, is not about age; it's not about a number; it's not morbid; it's not pessimistic; and it may even be funny. It is simply a question about lots of time passing, and when, exactly, did that happen?

What I have learned over these many years is that becoming a caregiver to parents definitely brings up this question. Looking at our own young adult children brings up this question. And sometimes looking in the mirror brings up this question. Getting older is something to think about, something to care about, something to cause us to initiate some planning related to the passing of time. Because time *is* passing; we are *not that* young; and we *may* be starting to face some of our own issues, outside of our parents', that are age-related.

The baby boomers, the largest segment of mid-life adults, are rather notorious for more reasons than simply their extremely large number. Many of us are not good planners and are not saving money. Many of us don't want to even think about the need for wills, estate planning, advance directives for health care, or changing our lifestyle habits in order to live a longer and healthier life.

We are very good at claiming how young we still are, how 60 or even 70 is the new 40, and talking about our latest successes at the gym – lifting heavier weights, longer time on the treadmill, looking better than ever. I am not saying there is anything wrong with this. It is, for the most part, a positive way to look at our lives. A close friend and I, both in our sixties, made a pact that we would, in some way important to each of us, now achieve our "personal best." Her area is music; mine is writing.

But I also believe that this optimism must be balanced with the reality that 60 is actually 60. We are starting to experience small, if not large, changes related to getting older, and it is extremely important to plan for our future years so that they are as abundant - physically, mentally, financially, emotionally and spiritually - as possible. We are all in this together, so let's talk about it.

The Conversation

In my interview, I asked the following questions about preparing for getting older. The questions are about balance, about planning, about change, about perspective. Here is the conversation.

Please sit in the circle and listen closely. And remember, these words are a continuous resource for you. You can always come back here, to this conversation, anytime you need wisdom, or support, or guidance. Your present experience may be different – but life constantly changes.

Question #1: What helps you the most in thinking about and preparing for your own aging?

Dawn: *A benefit from working in the aging field is that I have wonderful role models of people who have adapted to change and coped with losses. I have seen how I want to be and how I do NOT want to be. We all have role models – positive and negative – that we can look to and decide how we want to be.*

Terry: *In my work, I see aging all of the time. I'm so immersed in it and involved in it that I know the issues and can be better prepared. I look at all of these people that I see everyday who are 80 or 90 – they're not climbing mountains but they are enjoying life. They are enjoying a good meal, a good bottle of wine, a good concert.*

Patsy: *Having seen my own parents going through the aging journey—and understanding that it is the circle of life—gives me a sense of peace about aging. It is also hugely supportive having people in the same age group going through these same things. It is good to have friends who can laugh with you about aging things.*

Dawn: *I now understand what is valuable and meaningful – family, friends, a nurturing support system. I also understand that I do not want to put any restrictions on my kids in terms of decisions they make about me.*

I don't want to limit their decisions, causing a greater burden. I trust that they will make good decisions.

I am over 60 years old and know to dwell on the good things – and trust that I will remember to do that as I age. I have built great relationships in my life – a wonderful husband and kids and many friends.

Ellis: *Spirituality helps me cope with the journey of time passing. By helping others with their journey, I have learned that you don't need to be on the journey alone. I can ask for help. I have to make a concerted effort to reach out.*

Of course, on the practical side, I have to take care of my health through exercise and nutrition.

Peter: *My belief in God and having the closeness of my wife helps me as I think about getting older. I also know that my children will come through for me in the end, which is a comforting sign that I have raised them well.*

Kathi: *What helps me as I think about aging is reading, traveling, and always being open to experiencing new things. It is really important to reach for new things, whether it is relationships, moving to a new place – and not being afraid, always open to new possibilities. I say to keep a sense of adventure and a commitment to really wanting to make a difference.* ***Whatever walk I will be walking, I want to be making a positive difference. I am not afraid.***

Question #2: In what ways have you changed over the years?

Mike: *I have a stronger appreciation of the values of reasonable health, quality of health. Again, I don't sweat the small stuff. I appreciate my wife more than I ever have – even though she does not do yard work or housework, she is extremely gifted at making arrangements for going out to dinner.*

Dawn: *Priorities change. I value family and friends more than material goods. But I still do love to shop!!*

Patsy: *I now have a "joy of life" perspective and I more fully understand the importance of making a contribution to the world. On a personal note, I spend more time with my grandson.*

Ellis: *I have come to understand what my dad taught me – the importance of learning to let the world come to you rather than you shaping the world. He always said, don't let your knowledge of what 'could be' hamper the joy of today.*

Kathi: *I now see the value of humane endeavors as being more important than the glamour of the performing arts. I was always about the arts and looked down on people who were not involved in them in some way. I have really gone through a paradigm shift, realizing that the humane aspect is more important for our world. Especially for me, becoming aware of the awful ways that we treat animals, I highly respect people our age who are doing good things to save the world – doing good for people, for animals, for the earth.*

Terry (ever so practical): *I try to express appreciation more in all areas of my life. Also, I drink better wine.*

Question #3: If you could go back 30 years, what, if anything, would you do differently?

Patsy: *I would be much better about protecting my skin and start using moisturizers much earlier.*

Mike: *I would do two things differently. 1) I wouldn't have worked as much, and 2) I wouldn't have abused my body as much (smoking, drinking, etc.). In my late twenties to late thirties, I lived a hard life. I worked pretty hard and would do anything to achieve success – which included red eyes, and drinking with people that I couldn't stand.*

Peter: *I would not take life so seriously. I would be more carefree and try to enjoy it more. I would have been there to love and give to my parents. I would be a better husband, being more intimate, more appreciative, caring for her even when I don't agree with her.*

Terry: *For me personally, it would be better for me to say what's on my mind rather than letting something fester. But you have to find a way to do that in a non-threatening and hopefully a constructive way. I admire those who have an ability to do that.*

Dawn: *I wish I had spent more time concentrating on giving my children an enriched childhood. I didn't realize or appreciate how short the time would be. We just lived our lives, and the children came along for the ride. I would have been more intentional in raising them and given them good experiences.*

Peter: *My biggest regret is that I would have been with my kids more, doing things with them, sitting on the floor with them. I was always worried about my career and focusing on myself.*

Terry: *I would have wanted to spend more quality time with the kids. It's hard to define those quality situations, though. Sometimes we would go to an activity with our kids, thinking it would be quality time, that then we wouldn't have that much fun. So was that quality time?*

Patsy: *I would be much kinder to people in their fifties and sixties that I worked with. I wasn't unkind, but I wasn't sensitive to their issues. They may have been worrying about younger people passing them by or wondering what retirement would be like – my worries now.*

Also, and I think about this a lot – I would spend a million hours with my parents to learn about their history. I would have listened more. I was too busy doing. I would have really paid attention more to what was going on. And I would have saved more things from my own past.

Dawn: *I would have written down stories about my parents as they happened. Now, it is difficult to remember all that should be written down.*

The following final answers from two of our mid-life Cast are quite remarkable. I wish that I felt this same way. I often think about desired "do-overs."

Kathi: *Other than if I had been independently wealthy, I would not do anything differently. I am just one of those people who was meant to be single. There are some women who are resentful or bitter, but I just like to do my own thing. I have a lot of male friends and had some nice boyfriends – but maybe I am just too selfish. I am comfortable in my situation, and with the same resources, would live my life exactly the same way.*

Ellis: *I would not do anything differently. I feel so lucky. My dad gave me permission to "learn to live my life creatively, and to find joy in what I do."*

Lessons Learned

So what do we learn from this first conversation? What new perspectives can result from pondering the question, *"When did we get this old?"*

New Priorities

What speaks to me most clearly is that people change their priorities and their perspectives. This leads to a vastly healthier outlook about not being so young anymore. It's kind of a "wisdom thing." Stronger appreciation for health, family, friends, relationships, humane endeavors, (and even drinking better wine!) can and does diminish the negative concepts associated with getting older—and maybe diminishes the fear that we all have, to some extent, of moving into our later years. It is a little like the "quantity vs. quality" debate. In mid-life, the quantity of years before us is probably fewer than of those behind us. But if we embrace the change of focus that does come with wisdom, the quality of those years might be better than ever.

When we can drop the negative images and appreciate the new priorities that can come with being older – relationships over climbing the corporate ladder, freedom from commitment to rules, the capacity to listen and embrace over doing and judging, and kindness in almost all situations – then we can realistically accept being not old, but simply older, and focus on how we want to live the rest of our lives. We can celebrate family and friends, discover an enriched spirituality, and have the courage to take on new experiences. Sounds like a great life, doesn't it?

Role Models

The conversation emphasizes looking to role models as one way to improve how we live the rest of our lives. I believe an important corollary to that is to become a role model for our children and other younger adults and be an example of living life fully at any age.

My daughter, at the ripe old age of twenty-something, asked herself, "*When did I get this old?*" What happened to high school, to college? She then decided to get on a plane and move to New York. She is an adult – what happened to her childhood? It flew by! Now in my sixties, my job is to set an example for her by constantly creating new memories in my own life so that she understands how the years just keep on coming and they just keep bringing new opportunities. We can't grab on to time and stop it – we can't put time in a bottle. Even if we could, would we really want to?

Do-overs or Do Better Now?

The final piece of this particular conversation that asks, **What would you do differently?** may seem like a frivolous question since we can't stop or go back in time. We can't put life in reverse and spend more time with our kids. We can't completely "un-damage" damaged skin. We can't go back to the workplace and change things after we retire. But, we can move forward in life with the knowledge of what we would have done differently. We can apply that knowledge to how we take care of ourselves now, how we treat others, how we build relationships, how we set aside time to write things down and/or to simply be still.

Most importantly, we can use this knowledge, this awareness, and share, *share*, **share** with those that are following us. Whether we would do many things differently or, like some, not do anything differently at all – this is vital for younger people to hear, even if they don't seem to be listening.

It *IS* the "wisdom thing" – and it matters.

Key Learning Points

- As mid-life adults, the often-asked question, *When Did We Get This Old?!?* causes us to recognize the passing of time and realistically plan for how we want to best live our older years.

- A focus on relationships, role models of successful aging, recording our memories and listening to others with an open heart can celebrate the quality of life over the quantity of years.

- It is crucial to share with those who are following us in time about our mistakes, about our successes, and about our newly-found wisdom about living life with courage and optimism.

Time for Writing and Reflection

1. Ask yourself, no matter what age you are, *When Did I Get This Old?* Write down your first responses to what this question brings up for you. Is it Sad? Reflective? Resentful? Humorous? What are your stories?

2. Think and write about what your input would be to the questions in the dialogue of this chapter – What helps you? Changes you have made? What would you do differently?

3. Gather a small group of friends/acquaintances and have an honest discussion about the changes, fears, hopes and dreams of the older years of life. Find elements of joy, optimism and humor – lift each other up! Enjoy!!

12

Laughing at Ourselves: The Gift of Humor
Our Continued Conversation

"I would wear clothes in the shower if I could,

but I probably wouldn't get very clean."

~My sister, Jonelle

The most important aspect of navigating through the mid-life years may be the ability to keep a sense of humor. Yes, it is important to discover how to prepare for our older years, shift our priorities, and gather the wisdom to help the generations that are following us. But do you really want to know the truth?? If we can laugh – *really, really laugh* – we will enjoy life's journey to its fullest!

When, during a conversation that we were having about our changing looks, my sister Jonelle made the above "shower statement," we literally laughed until we cried. She is a very attractive mid-life woman, looking at least 10 years younger than she is. Plus she is tiny, fit, and bubbly.

However, and this is a big "however" for her and probably for most women and men over the age of 50 or 55, *things are changing*. She looks at her skin and it is not as firm, even with regular exercise. She looks at her legs and sees veins that didn't show before.

She looks at her hands and they are starting to look like our mother's. She looks at her face, but always wants pictures to be taken from a distance so that the wrinkles aren't the main attraction. She doesn't really enjoy looking at herself anymore. Thus, the statement, *"I would wear clothes in the shower if I could, but I probably wouldn't get very clean."* After we stopped laughing, I told her, *"Jonelle that is definitely going to be in my book!"* The perfect quote to begin my chapter on laughing at ourselves!

Before you start to think that this is a negative outlook on mid-life, let me say clearly that my sister is not depressed or discouraged. She is now retired after over 40 years of teaching; she knows she was one of the most popular teachers in her school. She is happily helping to take care of her five-year-old granddaughter and participates in a wide variety of interesting activities. Her form of exercise is aerobic dance, and she knows she looks really good in her later years of mid-life.

However, with passing years, our physical appearance and our physiology do start to change. We can spend our time worrying, and sometimes we do, but, of course, this is not helpful. Or we can find a better perspective, like sharing with friends of a similar age that we "want to take a shower with our clothes on," and laugh really hard. My sister and I could laugh – I am five years younger than she is, and I am ready to get into that shower with my clothes on.

I love to laugh and I'm sure you do too. But when it comes to some of the changes and losses that accompany aging, it can be very difficult to find the humor. Sometimes, it really is almost impossible. That's when it's time to share with others! And enjoy the laughter!!

When we find the freedom to laugh at ourselves, it is a powerful way to boost our mood, heal our anxieties about some unwanted changes that come with aging, and it can be a great way to uplift each other. Laughing at ourselves with others who share the same small but annoying signs of aging is definitely a gratifying shared experience. Laughing brings fresh perspective when we are wishing that we were young again.

A key motivation for writing this book was to share about how humor is such an important ingredient for graceful aging and effective caregiving. I have experienced *so much* humor throughout my long career in gerontology. So our Cast was asked first about laughter in the journey of caring for aging parents, which we explored in Chapter 5. As you will remember, there were many heartfelt and humorous stories. Then I asked them to come up with stories about laughing at themselves, which was easy for some and not so easy for others.

So here we are again, sitting in our support group circle, sharing funny experiences with getting a bit older. First, listen to our Cast and all of the humorous stories of their lives. Then, reflect on your own life. What are some of your stories? Think about which one you would share.

Here is the question from the interview:

Question: What is one humorous anecdote that you are willing to share about your own aging?

It's about the body.

Mike: *It's kind of a man thing. 90% of the people that I spend time with are life-long friends. We have experienced all of life's cycles together – first girlfriend, first "getting lucky," marriage, children, aging and the death of parents. When we go into the restroom, the conversation usually entails one of the following: having a problem getting started or having a problem knowing when you're done. We all look at each other and someone says, "I can't determine whether I'm having a problem getting started or stopping."*

Along those same lines is the following comment:

Terry: *Recently, I was with a colleague (who thankfully was also a good friend) and we were driving to our office in Los Angeles. I had had a second cup of coffee and I had to stop at a hotel even though we were only 10 minutes from the office. I haven't had that second cup of coffee since then! I may have to start thinking along the lines of 'incontinence can be fun!'*

And still about the body.

Dawn: *I joined a yoga class because it was supposed to be relaxing. It turned out not to be relaxing at all because my body would not do what I wanted it to. I laugh when I leave because the best part of the class is when it's over!*

And even more about the body.

Patsy: *What IS funny is that I look at my body and I say, "Who the hell is this?" Shopping for a bathing suit certainly brings this out. And I can't wear high heels anymore – I'll catch my heels in the cracks of the sidewalk, so I wear sensible shoes now. I would break my leg just trying on some of the shoes that young people wear.*

And ski stuff is now somewhat funny. In my head, I am jumping off the cornice – but I know that my body won't do that.

There are unique reasons to laugh.

Kathi: *I laugh because I actually worry about becoming a cat hoarder. I knew of an 80-year-old woman who had 47 cats in a one-bedroom apartment! She was trying to save cats. I am trying to save cats. I know there is a shred of truth that I could become the "cat lady." I will have to be really careful.*

But it's not always easy to laugh.

Ellis: *I make other people laugh, so I can laugh too. I am always losing things, and I'm messy. I spend a lot of time looking for things. At work, I got up and started to walk and I still had headphones on – the wires got tangled all over and wrapped around me.*

Another time, I had my headphones plugged into the wrong hole so the music was blaring out so that everyone could hear.

Sometimes I wear my clothes inside out. I don't put things in specific places – I had to go to Barnes and Noble three times because I kept forgetting my wallet.

I have always been this way, but maybe it's true that as we get older, we become more of what we already are. I do make other people laugh – and even though to me it's not always funny, when they laugh, I can laugh, too. I need people around me who will help me with these things and help me laugh.

Patsy: *One thing that others think is funny (but I don't) is when I have "senior moments." My mind goes blank and I can't remember numbers as well. At council meetings, I like to have the answer right away, but the answer isn't always accessible anymore. I tell them I will have to get back to them. Now, I can't crank out the numbers as I used to. I have to make cheat sheets which is very hard for me. This experience is still too close so it is not funny even though others think it's funny.*

Peter: *I can't laugh about getting older yet. It still makes me anxious. I'm trying to wipe off my age spots. They're bigger than four years ago.*

I believe what would help both Patsy and Peter to laugh about these small pieces of getting older is to share about senior moments, cheat sheets, and age spots with others of a similar age. After all, these are not life threatening conditions. When a friend or colleague relays the same experience, worry can become comedy. Patsy could give a knowing look to a colleague across the table that also has a cheat sheet – and they could quietly laugh.

And again there is the reassurance that we are all in this together, which lifts the burden a bit.

My Own Stories

Now that our Cast has each taken a turn, it is only fair that I share some of my own experiences in which laughter played a big role. After all, I'm part of the support group too!

I've had several conversations over the past months and years with family and friends in which after getting over the initial embarrassment, we've been able to enjoy the humor of our situation. I bet your have similar stories.

Unwanted Facial Hair

I was having lunch with a good friend and she started to tell me, somewhat seriously, that she had just had laser hair removal on her face. I asked about the location of the laser center and the technician, telling her that I should probably do that too. When she asked why - my facial hair is blonde so not as noticeable as some - I told her that every time I go in for a pedicure (something that used to be a luxury but has become a necessity – when did I get these dry feet?) - the woman who does the waxing in the salon always comes running up to me with her waxing tools in hand and immediately shows me all of my facial hair issues. I told my friend that I was thinking about titling this chapter, "Attack of the Wax Woman."

In some way, because of that shared experience of unwanted facial hair that has decided to grow in our mid-life, it became funny. The more we talked about hair, waxing, lasers, making sure our daughters know to let us know if we have missed a bad one, the funnier it got. We still laugh about it, and check with each other about how the facial hair thing is working out. I haven't done laser, yet, I'm rather afraid of it. I just keep waxing away!

Incidentally, in preparation for a recent trip to Hawaii, I went in for a pedicure. Guess who showed up right by my chair within a few minutes? Yes, the Wax Woman!

Our Beauty Routines

Another good friend and I were having a conversation about how we spend our time these days. She made the comment that it is a "full-time job" just getting ourselves ready for the day and looking somewhat attractive. She began to enumerate all of the steps we take to come out with a finished product that is acceptable to us. First there are moisturizers for face, body, and feet. We need sun block, foundation make-up, subtle eye make-up that enhances the color of our eyes, but distracts from the wrinkles. And of course we have to choose clothes that are flattering and discreetly hide body areas that are not as firm as they used to be. We don't even get a break at night. There are the nighttime creams for deep moisture, wrinkle removal, and puffy eyes. It takes a lot of time!! Plus we go to the hair stylist far more often because we are still not quite ready to go grey – another time consuming activity.

The problem is that we have other stuff to do – like work! But for those of us who do care about how we look - and that is most people - we have to laugh at ourselves as we go through all of these steps. We are not our daughters who can roll out of bed, throw on sweats, put their hair up in a messy bun, not put on any make-up, run out the door and still look beautiful. If we went out like that, the people we encounter would ask about our health! My friend and I had a good laugh as we shared our "beauty steps" – and guess what? We decided to keep our "full-time job" because we both still look pretty damn good!! And that happens to be important to us.

And men – it's not so easy for you either! You may not have the make-up and hair issues, but I would guess that many of you might have hair growing in unwanted places that requires some careful removal. And the fitness/physique issue definitely becomes a more time consuming endeavor. In addition to regular exercise, you are very likely similar to my husband who has to spend as much time stretching as exercising. Why? Bad back, sore shoulders, stiff legs. The upside for him is that he now gets to watch all of those interesting programs that are on TV at 5:30 a.m. as he does his morning stretches in order to get moving for the day.

Our Portable Pharmacies

Then there is the issue of medications, vitamins and supplements. Once, I was on a tour to Spain and Portugal with my two sisters and a close friend. The third morning, one of my sisters had a terrible allergic reaction - we still don't know to what - and her face was noticeably swollen and bright red. It was painful to look at! When she came into the lobby where the other tour members were waiting for the bus, practically every woman in our group immediately opened their purses and took out their rather large "medicine cache" looking for Benadryl or some sort of anti-histamine. It even made my sister laugh, in spite of her discomfort, as we all realized that amongst our 32 people on the tour, we were carrying an entire pharmacy!

The late Nora Ephron, a world-renowned author, screenwriter, and director, refers to this phenomenon in her most recent book, *I Remember Nothing*. She shares with us in a joking manner that you know you are older, or at least "oldish," when the amount of pills you take in the morning doesn't leave room for breakfast. This certainly seemed true – and funny – for our "oldish" tour group. And the good news for my sister is that she got the anti-histamine that she needed!

Physical Challenges

A few years back, I ran into an old high school friend at the JFK airport in New York. I was there because I had just arrived to help my daughter move to New York City. He was there to run the New York City marathon. We are the same age so I was pretty impressed that he was planning to run the marathon. When I expressed my admiration that he was going to run 26 miles, he laughed and said, *"This will be my last one – my knees are killing me! And I've had all kinds of injuries during my training. But I've done 10 marathons before, and my business partner and I both said we would do the New*

York marathon when we turned 60." Then we laughed together. It was that shared "being in our sixties" experience. He appeared to be in excellent shape, and I'm sure he will continue to pursue physical endeavors – just not 26 miles of them. I wish I could have seen him after the race to hear his story. I'm sure it was funny! I'm also sure he finished!

And speaking of knees, a family friend who is also in his sixties recently had knee replacement surgery. His recovery was a little tough because he is used to being constantly active. But after a few months, he is feeling fine and is back to normal activity. As he talks about his experience, he laughs and shares this – *"Life is like a roll of toilet paper and we are getting really close to the cardboard."* Maybe not so profound – but very funny!

Braces in Mid-Life?

Then there's my dear friend Joann, my personal choice for "Daughter of the Year" because of her complete devotion to her mother. She has gone back to school to become a medical technician. After she explains via email the difficulty of the program, and how the other students are younger and have more medical background, she adds a P.S. which says, *"My bottom teeth have shifted, even though a permanent wire was glued on the back. I may have to wear braces on the bottom teeth. Real cute . . . an old lady going back to college with braces!"* I can hear her laughing as she writes this.

To Sleep Together or Not?

Last fall, we were visiting some close friends and went out for a nice dinner. Somehow the conversation turned to snoring. Yes, snoring! We were comparing volume, pitch and unusual sounds. As the various types of snoring were discussed, and the consequences of loud snoring were shared, we all began to laugh uncontrollably. It turns out that the husband of my close friend often gets sent to the extra bedroom. At the same time, she got the award for the most high-pitched and strange-sounding type of snore. As for my husband and myself, we have been pretty gentle with each other when it comes to snoring. But with this hilarious conversation, we found a new freedom to do what it takes to get a good night's sleep.

Those Pesky Senior Moments

Probably the most difficult thing to laugh about is memory loss. I think we all fear, on some level, the possibility of losing our memory. People laugh about it all the time though. We make remarks about going into a room to get something and then not being able to remember what it is that we were going to get, opening the refrigerator for something that's in the pantry, constantly looking for keys or glasses, forgetting names and events, writing notes in order to remember and then losing the notes. We even make jokes about having Alzheimer's.

Most people laugh at these things, but I think we bring them up a lot because we are looking for reassurance from others that we are just normally forgetful and not slipping into memory loss and dementia. Those "senior moments" can be a little bit unsettling, especially if there is a history of Alzheimer's in the family. We want to hear that our friends are experiencing the same thing. And they are. It feels good to laugh about it. It feels great to laugh about it.

There *is* a certain amount of normal age-related forgetfulness and it has nothing to do with Alzheimer's. It is said in gerontology that this is the difference. If you keep misplacing your keys, you are somewhat forgetful and distracted and need to set up a system to always keep your keys in the same place. If you forget what your keys are for and put them in the refrigerator, then you may have dementia and need to seek help.

Most of us do not have dementia – at least not yet, and not for a long time. We forget more, but we also have more to remember, many years of things to remember. So let's laugh together when we can't remember the plot of a book that we read only a few months ago. After all, we have probably read a few books since then. The good news is that if we decide to re-read that book at some point, it will seem like we are reading it for the first time!

Closing Thoughts on Laughing at Ourselves

Laughter is powerful. Laughter boosts our mood. Laughter is healing. Laughter is a gratifying shared experience. Laughter can bring a fresh perspective when we are wishing that we were young again.

In closing this chapter on Laughing at Ourselves, I would like to again refer to the late Nora Ephron (1941 – 2012). She wrote two books that have much to say about laughter and getting older. The titles themselves are funny – *I Feel Bad About My Neck (2006)*, and *I Remember Nothing (2010)*. Her books deal with reflections on other issues, too, but getting older and finding humor in our ever-changing selves is certainly a prominent theme. She really knew how to laugh at herself. And she gives us an "out" for those pesky "senior moments." When we can't remember something, we can just Google it. So no more senior moments. Just Google moments. Much more current, right?? We can even impress our adult kids!

I heard Nora Ephron interviewed on a daytime talk show when she was promoting her most recent book, and she said something close to (and I am paraphrasing), *"Now that it is time to write my memoir, I remember nothing."* She was laughing – so were the co-hosts. At that time, she was 69 years old and certainly, in her writing, doesn't diminish the losses and concerns that come with aging. And of course, she didn't really "remember nothing." But she reminds us, with her extremely clever writing, that there is a humorous side to all of this getting older stuff. And I'm with her. I'm going to choose to keep laughing. Please join me.

Key Learning Points

- As we move through mid-life, it becomes increasingly important to recognize the humor that lies with in many age-related changes and be able to laugh out loud at ourselves.

- Sometimes, and especially for some people, the worry about physical changes and/or forgetfulness overcome the ability to laugh.

- An almost certain remedy for not being able to laugh at ourselves is to share with others of the same age and same experiences and then we may really, really laugh. We laugh together and lift each other up!

Time for Writing and Reflection

1. Brainstorm and make a list of the age-related changes that you are noticing. They may be physical changes, changes in how you think about life, or possibly changes in relationships.

2. As you think about these changes, identify and write about how you can find humor and reasons to laugh about these many changes.

3. Gather a group of family and friends to share stories that are age-related and potentially funny. Find common areas of humor and create an atmosphere in which you can all have the greatest time just laughing, even to tears!

13

Aging Gratefully:
Our Closing Conversation

"I am thankful for the example that my parents set of never valuing money above relationships."

~Ellis

When I had a physical a few years ago, I found out that something called an A1C, which I don't think I had heard of before, was above the normal range. Translation? Many of you probably know the answer. The beta cells in my pancreas are not fully doing their job. Translation again? I have too much sugar in my blood and am in that group on the chart identified as "pre-diabetic." Truthfully, I absolutely couldn't believe it! I am not overweight by any measure. I eat relatively healthy. I do the whole grains, less red meat, *close* to eight servings of fruits and vegetables a day. And I actually do exercise three to four times a week. I could certainly improve in all of these areas, but I think I am way above average in responsibly managing my health. Now I have this label of "pre-diabetic" and I hate it!

The Challenge to be Grateful

How does my pre-diabetic condition have anything to do with aging gratefully? You see, I was formulating this chapter more vividly in my mind when I received the above information, and I thought maybe I should just delete this chapter altogether. I felt so angry! I felt angry at the doctor for wanting me to take another pill, at my parents for giving me bad genes, at myself for making such a big deal out of it and acting like I had received a terminal diagnosis. And I was angry at the aging process. I wanted to be young again!

However, the interesting thing is that when I started creating this book in my head, my first imagined title was "Aging Gratefully." I knew that I wanted to present a somewhat different perspective on getting older, one that was based on gratitude, on joy, on laughter, on hope. So its surprised me that I was ready to toss out my one chapter specifically devoted to gratitude because my A1C was too high! Sometimes it is truly tough to be grateful.

Also, I have been intrigued by the concept of gratitude for a long time. Several years ago, I used to regularly listen to Dennis Prager on KABC talk radio. In his book *Happiness Is A Serious Problem*, he writes extensively about gratitude and calls it the key to happiness. As I reflected on that premise, I decided that I believe that. I believe that wholeheartedly. How can we be unhappy if we are truly grateful for what we have?

Naturally Grateful

Oftentimes we are just naturally full of gratitude. Maybe it's an engagement, a long-anticipated grandchild, a particularly special family gathering, a new relationship, satisfying work or satisfying retirement, or simply being alive on a beautiful day. For me, the other night, it was listening to Beethoven's 7th at the Walt Disney Concert Hall, conducted by the dynamic, yet ever so humble, Gustavo Dudamel. I was jumping out of my seat with joy and gratitude to give a lengthy standing ovation to the beauty and genius that exists in our world! Sometimes, it is so easy to be grateful.

Obstacles to Being Grateful

But the real truth is that with the passing of time, there are many things that stand in the way of gratitude. We have our physical issues, probably the number one source of complaint. Life is changing in ways that maybe we don't want it to. Maybe it's losing parents, children moving away, mixed feelings about retirement or possibly working for someone younger than us - changes that mean loss. So we complain, or we feel sad and discouraged. And there probably aren't many times when we are jumping out of our seats with joy, wildly applauding for all of the good things that are happening. Much of the time, you have to make a determined effort to express gratitude, to indeed, be grateful.

When I was in my twenties, I had a framed poster (yes, a poster) over my desk at work that said, "Happiness is like a butterfly. If you chase it, it will elude you. But if you sit quietly, it will alight on your shoulder." I'm not sure why I still remember that poster but

I think it's because that even in my twenties, I wasn't sure how to be happy. I always wanted something more fulfilling in my job. I was looking for that relationship that would become permanent. I was always trying to be a bit thinner. I was still trying to prove to myself and to others that I was smart and capable. I wasn't particularly happy, and definitely not grateful for all that I already had and for the opportunities that were before me. I was always trying harder, but for what though, I don't know.

Now I know, after much reflection, that in these great years of mid-life, that we have to make a *conscious decision* to do those things that foster happiness. A cliché about butterflies is not going to work. We might have to chase that butterfly after all. If we sit quietly and wait for happiness to alight on our shoulder, it may eventually work, but we will probably be waiting for a very long time. We have to pursue happiness with vigor and courage! A grateful heart will help us capture those happy moments and lead to a happier life, even in the face of passing years.

So I challenge you, whether you are 20, 40, 60, 80 or older, to focus on those things for which you can be grateful. Think about them. Write them down. Meditate on them. Record your reasons to be grateful and erase that tape that plays continuously in your head that recites your reasons to complain and be unhappy. Let's take this challenge together. I could use the help.

As we begin our journey toward gratitude, let's turn first to our Cast and listen to their reasons for being grateful. This is the final session of our support group. Let's listen and then see if we can help each other discover how to focus on that sometimes evasive quality called gratitude.

Here is the question from the interview:

Question: What are the five things for which you are most grateful?

Mike: *My wife, my children, the fact that I have been able to maintain a close-knit family where we all take care of each other, friends, and my dog.*

Terry: *Family. I have a good life (living in the U.S. and not a third world country), so we are economically able to have a good quality of life. We have the resources to maintain contact across geographies and are easily able to travel. The networking that has come through church – my parents had this and I see it as having value for me in the future. For me, work can be aligned with personal values.*

Dawn: *I made a good choice in a life partner – we have grown together, not apart. I had wonderful parents and a good childhood. I live in a country of freedom. I have lived long enough to see my children become responsible adults and have the joy of grandchildren. Good health as of now – I enjoy life without limitations.*

Patsy: *Parents who were good to me so I had no reason not to be good to them. The shared experience with my siblings while taking care of my mother. My husband and son – Patrick was young while mom was aging, but it creates an odd balance in your life. It is very demanding, but also healthy – you don't get stuck in one world, young or old. Living in a community with a lot of resources – I am grateful for what I chose to be* *professionally and how it has affected and helped my personal life. And good friends – long term friendships. Family is where you go to at night and they've got to let you in. It may not be a blood relative. I have a lot of people in my life that would "let me in" at midnight.*

Kathi: *The safety and security that my parents provided when I was a child, my faith in Christ, my health, my friends, my career.*

Peter: *God, my wife, my children, my health, and being financially secure so that I can take care of my family.*

Ellis: *My parents and the transmittal of their value that you can do anything that you want. Being able to live the value of "doing unto others as they would do unto you."* **I am thankful for the example that my parents set of never valuing money above relationships.** *The courage to look foolish and make mistakes. The understanding that it takes time and commitment to build a loving family. A profession that I love.*

Sources of Gratitude

You will immediately recognize that each person first stated something about relationships – spouse, children, parents, God. For Mike, relationships summed up the entirety of the five things for which he is most grateful. His answers were spontaneous and immediate. He didn't have to think about it at all. This is coming from someone who is highly successful financially – but he never mentioned a beautiful home, a nice car, or money in the bank.

If you read through the responses again, you will also recognize that other sources of gratitude emanate from an idea of relationship – love of country, freedom, faith, community, networking, sharing of values, commitment, professions that align with values and principles, courage, safety, security. All of these are about relationship with others and with ourselves. For those who mentioned gratitude for good health, it was about allowing them to live freely and without limitation in relationship to the people they love.

Peter, the youngest of the mid-life adults, did emphasize financial security. But notice, he didn't say that he was grateful that he has lots of money. He spoke of finances in terms of security—the security to be able to take care of his family. Relationships.

Roads to Gratitude

As we spoke about gratitude in the interviews, some had advice for others. They gave advice for you, for me, younger and older, to live a more grateful life. Peter encourages us to build a community of support. He says that as we get older, we need that support. We need other people as a foundation so that we can laugh and cry together. I agree! And this isn't necessarily about "blood relatives." This community may very well be friends or colleagues—people that we have chosen to spend our time with. People who share a history with us. People who accept us for exactly who we are. A community of support can help us in those difficult times when we feel angry or sad or discouraged, and help us to arrive at a place of acceptance and maybe even gratitude.

Kathi and Ellis are both adamant about the importance of finding your passion and following your dreams as you pursue a grateful life. Ellis says, *"Choose a profession that you love and are passionate about."* And Kathi says it this way: *"Go with your dreams. Go where your passion is. Then, you will find the path. There are no guarantees, but if you go with your passion, not primarily in relation to financial gain, you'll find the way."* These are roads to gratitude; gratitude is a clear road to happiness.

This is not only advice for younger people who are looking for a career path, it is great advice for those of us in mid-life and beyond, too. We are still vital. As we've talked about, maybe we are looking for that Second or Third Act—a new career, a volunteer opportunity, a new relationship, a creative outlet, or ways to strengthen family ties. Whatever it is, let's follow the advice of Kathi and Ellis, and choose not what we think we should do, but that which we really want to do – a passion, a dream. This will surely keep us on the path of gratitude.

I have to admit that sometimes I have a gratitude relapse. I'll wake up in the middle of the night and feel sad that I am not yet a mother-in-law or a grandma when almost all of my friends are. Or I will dwell on the past and make a mental list of all of the mistakes that I have made. I am inclined to notice my physical flaws and yearn to be young again. I compare myself to extremely accomplished people and wonder if I have made a significant contribution to this world.

When I have these negative thoughts, I have to make that conscious decision to open my mind and heart to gratitude. Yes, gratitude is knocking at my door. Then I can remember that I had wonderful and loving parents; that I have three beautiful, smart, successful children; that I have devoted my life to the field of gerontology; that I have been happily married for 40 years; and that I have an amazing group of intelligent, gorgeous and successful friends. Reasons to be grateful – and happy.

Closing Thoughts on a New Gratitude

I am compelled to end this chapter with Terry's advice for looking at our lives and being grateful. He is always practical and to the point. As he talks about how to live life gratefully, he gives this advice: *"Enjoy life! There are different things that you can get enjoyment out of when you are older. Find out what those are. What you find enjoyment in as you age will be different from 20 years ago. Things that you enjoy evolve. Recognize that and go with that. An example for my wife and me is that we enjoy a whole day preparing for having a dinner party with friends."* And you can bet that they serve good wine!

And, speaking of wine let me go back to my A1C dilemma. I may have to change my eating habits just a bit and exercise one day more a week. And maybe I will add a pill to my array of vitamins and supplements. But I am told by a good friend who is a dietitian that I do not need to give up my two favorite drinks - coffee and wine. In fact, in some wonderfully weird twist of fate, coffee and wine are actually beneficial for people with high blood sugar – in moderation, of course.

Now, that's something to be grateful for! Aging gratefully.

Key Learning Points

- When faced with the changes and losses that often come with being in mid-life, it can be difficult to feel grateful, which in turn lessens our happiness.

- It is essential to focus on those aspects of our lives, especially the relationships that we enjoy, for gratitude to become an integral part of our daily experience.

- We can learn to appreciate new activities, pursue new adventures and make more time for our family and friends, which will put us on the road to gratitude and to happiness.

Time for Writing and Reflection

1. Write down the 5 things for which you are most grateful. Feel free to add as many as you want.

2. Take the gratitude challenge. Erase the negative tape that plays continuously about reasons to be unhappy and replace it with all of the many reasons to be grateful, big and small.

3. Start a gratitude journal. Write about those things for which you are grateful each day. You may want to focus on one particular area of gratitude or you may just want to list as many as you can for that day. Enjoy!

14

Artichokes and Grace
Some Final Thoughts on Aging

— ♥ —

I have thought about aging more than most people.

Gerontology became my profession when I was just 22 years old. Now I am 66. That is a lot of years to think about aging – and not only to think about it, but to actively be involved in, pretty much, "all things aging."

I have worked with hundreds of older people and their families at the vulnerable time of possibly needing supportive housing and care.

I have been, many times over, a professional and personal support to older people as they make difficult choices and changes.

I've had lots of fun with older people. A great memory is directing a choir with the average age of my singers being about 85. We were terrible – but we all loved it! So did our audience!

I have studied aging, taught aging, given speeches on aging. I even participated in experiential learning (you know, Vaseline on the glasses, walking around blindfolded) when I was only in my twenties in order to try to "understand" what it might be like to be older. This is probably a very outdated method of teaching, but it was effective for me at the time. I went from taking that class to teaching that class.

I have held many hands in the final moments of life, and sat with many families in their grief.

I have lost both parents, and I am getting pretty close to becoming my own client.

And now, I have had the extraordinary privilege of talking to others and recording in this book their thoughts about aging parents and their own aging.

Yes, I have thought about aging more than most people.

So with what do I leave you, dear reader? Good question. Hard question. Ultimately, I have a simple answer. I am going to leave you with a story about *artichokes*, my favorite food, and *grace*, my favorite word. And I do have the last word.

Artichokes – the Difficult But Delicious Vegetable

Artichokes are a very difficult vegetable. From the outside, they can look a little menacing, like a form of cactus or something, with those sharp needle-type points at the top end of each leaf. You have to be careful when you buy artichokes at the grocery store so you don't prick your fingers on the sharp points, and also so those sharp points don't rip through the plastic bag that you've placed them in causing your artichokes to fall on the floor. You have to really want artichokes to buy them.

When it is time to cook them you have two choices. You can leave the sharp points on and then you need to be very careful as you take off each leaf for your eating pleasure so that, again, you don't prick yourself. Or, you can laboriously cut the tops off each leaf before cooking so that when you finally get to eat your artichoke, you're not worrying about those prickly ends. My mother always left the sharp points on – maybe she didn't have time to cut them off. I have chosen to take the time to cut off the ends, carefully. We are all different.

The process of eating an artichoke is also a bit difficult. As you pull off each leaf, the top part is hard and grainy, and you are left scraping off the very bottom tip of the leaf, called the *bract* (yes, it has a name), with your teeth. Oh, but that bract tastes pretty good, especially if you dip it in butter or mayonnaise. It tastes good enough to pull off the next leaf, and the next, and the next. Then you begin to discover, as you are working your way to the more internal part of the artichoke, that you have more bract and less hard, grainy stuff. This is going well. Each delicious morsel of bract melts in your mouth.

There is still a problem, though. As you are savoring the taste of the bract, possibly closing your eyes to focus solely on the taste, you are building up a pile of rather unsightly leaves, with teeth marks across the bottom. So you want to be sure to have a nice separate bowl on the table in which to place the used leaves rather than to let them overtake your plate.

Now you are almost to the very middle of the artichoke, thoroughly enjoying your buttery bites. But the leaves suddenly become papery thin, very purplish, and the bract is miniscule. Even worse, when you pull off these pathetic looking leaves, underneath there is a mound of a fuzzy, furry, inedible substance called the *choke* (yes, it has a name too – a rather ironic one, don't you think?). Time to quit eating the artichoke? Add the rest to the bowl of previously eaten leaves to throw away?

For some people, yes – they just give up. Throw it away; add it to the compost. But for others, the persistent ones, they get a medium-sharp knife, and carefully scrape out the choke. It may take some time, because the choke likes to stick to the base. But as you put that last clump of furry choke in the bowl with the teeth-scraped leaves, you have uncovered the most delicious part of the artichoke – the heart. No more prickly ends, no more hard, grainy leaves, no more suspicious furry stuff – just a meaty, tasty, delectable round heart. It seems as though much of the bract has secretly descended to the bottom of the artichoke and formed this purely delicious surprise for us to delight in. You can pour butter all over it as you eat your prize – or it is delicious on its own.

Either way, as you slowly eat the artichoke heart, savoring each bite, the word that comes to mind is *grace*. The heart of the artichoke is grace – a near-perfect center within a rather difficult exterior. It is so delicious; it gives us a sense of well-being, of total satisfaction. You want to just sit at the table for a few more minutes, tasting the taste, marking the moment, sighing the sigh of contentment. You forget all about the prickly edges, the hard and grainy leaves, the furry stubborn stuff. You are experiencing the grace of the artichoke, the sheer joy of sensory delight, the feeling of contentment that comes with knowing that, for this moment, life is just grand.

Hold on to the thought of this experience. We'll come right back to it, as you probably suspect...

Lessons Learned from the Artichoke

So it's time for me to share a few final thoughts on aging, on the passing of time, on the question *"When did we get this old?"*

Life, especially as we get older, is oftentimes full of prickly edges and other difficult stuff – just like the artichoke. We find ourselves taking care of aging parents, not always knowing how to do that very well. We grieve their loss and wonder, *"Could I have done a better job?"*

We can be surprised, frustrated and ultimately sad about the changes that are taking place in our own lives – aging parents, children growing up, work transitions, health issues, not-so-youthful appearances. It's kind of like that hard, grainy stuff that turns into a pile of unsightly leaves.

We can almost be overwhelmed when we encounter an obstacle, a defining moment, a big furry clump that shifts the balance of our lives – with our aging parents or within ourselves.

So what can we do?

We can savor the delicious morsels of joy with our parents: A parent thanking us for helping. A confused parent's moment of clarity. A good decision related to care and well-being. A reason to laugh. A gentle touch. A warm hand. A peaceful death. A celebration of life.

And we can savor our own morsels of joy: A good workout. A new endeavor. Adult children successfully growing up. Strengthening old relationships and building new ones. Accepting a compliment. Giving a compliment. Discovering creativity. Enjoying a beautiful day or a glass of good wine.

And as we savor these morsels of *Joy*,
    we will experience *GRACE*.

GRACE that gives us contentment.

GRACE that fills us with a sense of peace.

GRACE that causes us to laugh out loud.

GRACE that allows us, when we ask the question, "When Did We Get This Old?" not to panic, not to long for the past, not to feel only loss and sadness, but to smile and be grateful for the present.

GRACE that gives us the wisdom to value life more than ever, and move forward with the excitement of knowing there is still much to experience of Joy, of Laughter, of
Gratitude, and of Hope.

Epilogue

Resources for Learning and Action

*R*esources about aging are abundant. So abundant, in fact, that it can be difficult to know where to start when you begin your quest for helpful information. To give you a starting point, I have put together a selected list of websites, organizations, associations and agencies, and books in my library that will launch you on your way to finding options and solutions for your parents and for yourself. I've included a brief description of the websites and the associations, etc. , – the book titles speak for themselves.

Remember – this list is just a starting point. These resources will likely lead you in additional directions that will further equip you to make well-informed decisions about "all things aging."

Resources for Act I – About Aging Parents

These are resources for your aging parents and for you, the caregiver.

Websites

www.ageinplacetech.com – Will keep you updated on a wide variety of technologies available to connect older adults and caregivers. Includes extensive information on new technology for dementia care.

www.agetek.org – An aging technology alliance of multiple companies that provides awareness of the vast array of tech products available for older people. A product finder will lead you to information on these products.

www.aginginplace.com – Provides help and information so that older adults can live safely and independently as long as they want in the home of their choice.

www.ahrq.gov/questionsaretheanswer/ - Lists the important questions that older adults should ask their doctor.

www.caring.com – A website for caregivers. It is designed to simplify caregiving and support caregivers. In addition to providing a wealth of information, it offers self-care tips for caregivers. Experts are available online to answer your questions.

www.eldercare.gov – A public service of the U.S. Administration on Aging, the eldercare locator will connect you to aging services in your community.

www.grandcare.com – The website for GrandCare Systems, a technology company that has developed, among a multitude of high tech products, a unique remote monitoring system that assists with long distance caregiving.

www.householdproducts.nlm.nih.gov/ - Provides information about the health effects of what is kept under the kitchen sink and other household products.

www.medicare.gov - The comprehensive government website for all issues related to Medicare.

www.medlineplus.gov – A service of the U.S. National Library of Medicine and the National Institutes of Health that will lead you to trusted and comprehensive health information. There is a specific tab for information on senior health issues. Drugs and herbal supplements are also included on this website.

www.newlifestyles.com – Connects you to senior living, care options, and products and services for older adults in your specific area.

www.nccam.nih.gov/timetotalk/ - Provides information that encourages discussion with your health provider about complementary and alternative medicine.

www.nihseniorhealth.gov – Specializes in health information for older adults. Incorporates senior-friendly features such as large text, sound, and contrast.

Associations, Organizations and Agencies

Aging Life Care Association – www.aginglifecare.org – An association of professionals in health and human services who help older adults and their families find and coordinate the appropriate services to meet their individual needs. The website will help you find an aging life care professional in your area.

Alzheimer's Association – www.alz.org – A nationwide association that provides an extensive array of information and services to persons with Alzheimer's and to their caregivers. The website includes research developments, housing and care information, opportunities for volunteer work and advocacy, and contacts for support groups in your area.

Cancer Support Community – www.cancersupportcommunity.org – An organization that provides psychological and social support to persons impacted by cancer through a network of nearly 50 local affiliates, more than 100 satellite locations, and online.

Family Caregiver Alliance – www.caregiver.org – As a public voice for caregivers, this organization provides information, education, services, research and advocacy to support family caregivers across the nation. They also publish fact sheets and publications on a wide variety of health and health-related topics that can be ordered online.

National Association of Area Agencies On Aging – www.n4a.org – The leading voice in government for aging issues. It administers the Eldercare Locator, listed above, which connects older adults and caregivers to appropriate resources in their communities. Another key program is a partnership with *Consumer Reports Best Buy Drugs* to assist older adults to make informed prescription drug decisions.

National Institute on Aging – www.nia.nih.gov – Supports and conducts research on health and aging. The institute provides an Information Center which can be contacted toll-free at 1-800-222-2225 or by email to niaiac@mail.nih.gov.

Social Security Administration – www.socialsecurity.gov – The public can receive information and apply for retirement and disability benefits on this website. Qualified older adults can also apply for Medicare Prescription Drug Cost Extra Help without making an appointment, calling or visiting.

Favorite Books in My Library

Berman, Claire. *Caring for Yourself While Caring for Your Aging Parent,* Third Edition. New York: Henry Holt and Company, 2005.

Delehanty, Hugh, & Elinor Ginzler. *Caring for Your Parents, The Complete Family Guide.* New York/London: AARP Sterling, 2008.

Fazio, Karen. *Care~Grieve~Grow, Caring For Your Aging Parents While Caring For Yourself.* Karen Fazio, 2013.

Henry, Stella Mora. *The Eldercare Handbook: Difficult Choices, Compassionate Solutions.* New York: HarperCollins, 2006.

Hogan, Paul and Lori. *Stages of Senior Care.* New York: McGraw-Hill, 2010.

Lebow, Grace & Barbara Kane. *Coping with Your Difficult Older Parent.* New York: HarperCollins, 1999.

Lustbader, Wendy. *Counting on Kindness.* New York: The Free Press, 1991.

Morris, Virginia. *How to Care for Aging Parents,* Third Edition. New York: Workman Publishing Co., 2014.

Russo, Francine. *They're Your Parents, Too! How Siblings Can Survive Their Parents' Aging Without Driving Each Other Crazy.* New York: Bantam Books, 2010.

Sheehy, Gail. *Passages In Caregiving: Turning Chaos Into Confidence.* New York: William Morrow, an imprint of HarperCollins, 2010.

Snelling, Sherri. *A Cast of Caregivers: Celebrity Stories to Help You Prepare to Care.* Indiana: Balboa Press, 2013.

Solie, David. *How to Say It to Seniors: Closing the Communication Gap with Our Elders.* New York: Prentice Hall Press, the Penguin Group, 2004.

Span, Paula. *When the Time Comes: Families with Aging Parents Share Their Struggles and Solutions.* New York: Springboard Press, 2009.

About Alzheimer's Disease

Because Alzheimer's disease is becoming a more important topic by the day, I am highlighting a few resources specifically to help you understand and cope with this disease.

Alzheimer's Association – www.alz.org – I am listing this resource again because I believe it is invaluable for pursuing all information on Alzheimer's Disease. This association/website will help you if you have the disease or if you are a caregiver for a loved one.

If you are concerned about a loved one who is wandering and may wander outside of the home, the Alzheimer's Association coordinates a nationwide I.D. program called "MedicAlert and Safe Return" which has a 24/7 helpline. To enroll, call 1-800-272-3900.

Alzheimer's Disease Education and Referral Center (ADEAR) – http://www.nia.nih.gov- Offers information and publications on research, diagnosis, treatment, patient care, caregiver issues, long term care, and other issues pertaining to optimal care for persons with Alzheimer's. The toll free number is 1-800-438-4380. Information on clinical trials is available.

Bell, Virginia and David Troxel. *The Best Friends Approach to Alzheimer's Care: A Guide for Care Partners.* Baltimore, Maryland: Health Professions Press, 2012.

Genova, Lisa. *Still Alice.* New York: Pocket Books, a Division of Simon and Schuster, Inc., 2009. (This is a work of fiction, but it realistically and sensitively portrays early on-set Alzheimer's disease).

Iris: A Memoir of Iris Murdoch (2001) – A movie, based on the book *Elegy for Iris* by John Bayley, a true story of English novelist Iris Murdoch's descent into Alzheimer's Disease. Available on DVD.

www.videocaregiving.org – A website of Terra Nova Films dedicated to providing a visual education center for caregivers of persons with Alzheimer's disease.

Resources for Act II – About Our Own Aging

The resources in this section are devoted to the concerns and aspirations of mid-life adults. Many of the websites listed for Act I, especially those devoted to medical concerns, also apply to mid-life adults. Please review those as well.

Websites

www.agewave.com – Website of the company Age Wave, devoted to providing an understanding of the effects of an aging population on the marketplace, the workplace and in our daily lives. The website will lead you to current research, consulting, publications and education concerning the aging phenomenon.

www.laughteryoga.org – Find a laughter yoga class near you that will help you to relieve stress and find joy in your daily life.

www.the3rdact.com – A website that will lead you to your unique way to design the rest of your life with passion, purpose and satisfaction.

Favorite Books in My Library

Bratter, Bernice and Helen Dennis. *Project Renewment: The First Retirement Model for Career Women.* New York: Scribner, 2013.

Donovan, Jim. *Take Charge of Your Destiny: How to Create the Life You Were Born to Live.* Jim Donovan, 2016.

Dychtwald, Ken and Daniel J. Kadlec. *A New Purpose: Redefining*

Money, Family, Work, Retirement, and Success. New York: Harper, 2009.

Ephron, Nora. *I Feel Bad about My Neck: And Other Thoughts on Being a Woman*. New York: Alfred A. Knopf, 2008.

Ephron, Nora. *I Remember Nothing: And Other Reflections*. New York: Alfred A. Knopf, 2011.

Genova, Lisa. *Still Alice*. New York: Pocket Books, Simon & Schuster, Inc., 2014.

Lustbader, Wendy. *Life Gets Better: The Unexpected Pleasure of Growing Older*. New York: The Penguin Group, 2011.

Rosenblatt, Roger. *Rules for Aging, A Wry and Witty Guide to Life*. San Diego, New York: Harcourt Books, 2001.

Sheehy, Gail. *New passages, mapping your life across time*. New York: Random House, 1995.

Happy Reading! Happy Research!!

Acknowledgements

— ❤ —

J have discovered over these past years that writing a book is certainly a long and winding road. It is also true that this road has multiple bumps, sharp curves, and dead ends. Occasionally the road is smooth and straight. But the writer's journey almost always takes a long time.

For me, writing *Artichokes and Grace* certainly followed this convoluted path. It is only with the help and support of those that I name here that I was able to get past the beginning, work through the middle, and finally achieve the end. To these people, I am eternally grateful.

The Beginning

It is because the mid-life adults, the Cast, were willing to share on a deeply personal level that I was able to develop the themes of this book. So my absolute resounding appreciation is for Dawn, Ellis, Kathi, Mike, Patsy, Peter and Terry. I thank them for their honesty, their willingness to express vulnerability, and their enthusiasm for the importance of sharing about aging parents and their own aging.

I also thank the supporting Cast that filled in the gaps and offered additional meaning to the narrative of the book. Alyce, Diana, Geri, Joann and Tom were vital to developing important themes about aging.

As I struggled to move beyond the first three chapters which I wrote over and over for longer than I want to admit, I am grateful for my young-adult reader, Ella Martin, who encouraged me to keep writing and gave me valuable feedback on each chapter until I reached the first version of the end.

At the same time, my son, Kevin, initiated an important "to do" list, which began with "Have a good conversation with Kevin." He helped to alleviate my anxiety over a process that included an immersion in social media. So I was able to move forward.

The Middle

My sincerest thanks goes to those that helped me as I embarked on the first major rewrite of my manuscript. Thank you, Robin Quinn, for your thorough evaluation of the manuscript. You helped me to raise the bar on my writing so that it would be worthy of publication.

This was a difficult time on the winding road of writing. I owe a huge thanks to my life-long close friends, Susan, Geri and Kathi for reminding me of the importance of what I was writing and not allowing me to give up. My husband and adult children were also key players in helping me to move through the sometimes tough and tedious work of rewrites and more rewrites. So thank you, my family — Steve, Erik, Kevin and Chelsea — for believing in me and pushing me to keep writing.

The End

And now, I have reached the end. My final proofreader, Julia Eddington, was thorough, thoughtful, and shares the love of the word "grace" with me. Thank you, Julia. Chelsea Buell, thank you for your extraordinary work on my website and on the graphic design for *Artichokes and Grace*.

And toward this "end," I want to express my deep appreciation to my son, Erik. He challenged me to keep writing when I was ready to give up. He took on the challenge to read my rewritten manuscript with the intent to make sure that I was clearly and concisely making my points – and that I wrote with a strong voice of personal experience and professional expertise. And he became my marketing/sales director— his strength, not mine.

And finally, I wish to thank all of the older adults and their families that I worked with over many, many years. They are the initial inspiration for writing about joy, laughter, gratitude and hope. May I now carry these forward into my own older years and live a life worthy of my favorite word – grace.

Praise for A&G

*A*rtichokes & Grace is a different kind of book about aging and caregiving. It's more than a "how to" book. The author integrates elements of interviews, knowledge and reality with a sacred philosophy of hope. The writing seamlessly takes the reader through joy and grief, pain and laughter, wisdom and forgiveness and ultimately gratefulness. And the writing is exquisite. Regardless of one's own life stage, this book gives you the opportunity to know more and feel "good" not only about your parents' aging, but also about your own—all within the context of reality. It's a must read.

~Helen Dennis, nationally recognized leader on issues of aging, employment and the new retirement, and co-author of The Los Angeles Times best-seller Project Renewment: The First Retirement Model for Career Women.

*I*n *Artichokes and Grace*, career gerontologist Kristen Falde Smith delivers the voices of adults who have stepped up to care for their aging parents. We see that though caregiving for parents can initially feel overwhelming, these individuals ultimately found it rewarding and doable while at times challenging. In addition, the caregivers share how they're approaching their own aging and the ways these experiences are influencing this. The author interweaves her own discernments and knowledge into the narrative with grace, wisdom and even humor. Rather than a how-to, the book is a well-written, insightful, heartfelt and at times playful reflection on the joys and sorrows of the aging of parents and us."

~Robin Quinn, Los Angeles editor and writer specializing in the book genres of self-help, health and spirituality, and producer and moderator of panels on publishing and writing issues throughout Southern California.

*K*risten Falde Smith artfully describes the joys and tribulations of accepting our own aging process while at the same time dealing with the demands of caregiving for aging parents. Through in-depth interviews and her own personal experience, she offers suggestions, reflections and recommendations for families and individuals experiencing this phase of life. Her writing is insightful and engaging and emphasizes the hope, joy, forgiveness and grace, which are necessary to care not only for our parents but for ourselves. Reading *Artichokes and Grace* reminds us of who we have become as a result of our parents, and reminds us that we always have a choice even in the most difficult of times."

~Ellis Waller, Professor at Coastline Community College, Huntington Beach, CA, recipient of the Betty and James E. Birren Emerging Leadership Award and a 2001 recipient of the California Virtual Campus Award for An Exceptional On-Line Course.

A must read . . . unless you don't expect to live another day. But if you do, immersing yourself in the stories, thoughts, emotions, and experiences cleverly and sensitively presented in Artichokes and Grace will make your understanding keener, your caring deeper, your patience more persevering, and your life richer. This read is a life-kaleidoscope in print . . . a sensitively crafted articulation of the oxymoronic journey we call aging . . . something we all do . . . each day as our eyes open once again, each night as they close, until that instant they open no more. *Artichokes and Grace* is like a finely polished mirror which reflects without distortion, an experienced and competent tutor invested in causing discovery of self and others, a powerful magnifying glass that makes accessible what is not obvious . . . but which is 'oh, so meaningful.' With unique gifts in observing, feeling, synthesizing, and exposing meaning, emotion, humor and inspiration in the midst of life's ambiguities, Kristen Falde Smith has patched for us a written quilt. Now wrap yourself in it and find warmth, softness, vibrant images that will sustain you in your own field trip into this world of aging, and sustain you, too, as you watch upon the field trips of others you know and love."

~Gary Wheeler, President of California Lutheran Homes, and former President and CEO of Front Porch, a nation-wide not-for-profit family of companies and services.

*I*n Artichokes & Grace, readers encounter voices from the front lines of respectful gerontological care. In her honest and optimistic voice Kristen Falde Smith expertly guides readers down the often rocky trails of both later-life care and aging with her own experience-tested knowledge and the stories of real caregivers. Smith addresses common difficulties and frustrations head-on and offers readers both empathy and concrete courses of action, which allow for grace, and even joy, during elder-caregiving and aging.

~Julia Eddington, editor and writer

A delightful read from an author who shares her professional and human insights into a subject that we all must face at some point. Her humor and pathos can help us all to face those difficult times and decisions.

~Christopher A. Scott LCSW, CGP, Village Counseling Center

About the Author

*K*risten Falde Smith has dedicated over 40 years of service to the field of gerontology. She earned her Master of Science degree in Gerontology (MSG) from the University of Southern California in 1978 and was a graduating member of the second-ever class in what was then, the newly created gerontology program. She is truly a "pioneer" in the field. She established her career in the not-for-profit, long-term care community. She served in a variety of positions in social services, community outreach, administration, governing boards, and in-service education and training related to ethics in the older years and at the end of life.

Through her variety of roles in long-term care, she gained extensive experience in many important areas within the field. She cherishes the many years of direct one-on-one interactions with older people and their families, gently guiding them in conversations and decisions about important life transitions, including end-of-life care. Her role as a senior administrator presented the challenge of providing the highest quality of care and service, while her time spent in ethics training focused on autonomy, respect and dignity.

This rich blend of her experience with older adults was the inspiration for writing Artichokes & Grace. Kristen believes that the sharing of stories and personal experiences is the most effective and engaging way to help others navigate the often difficult, but ultimately uplifting and joyful path of aging.

54455074R00200

Made in the USA
San Bernardino, CA
17 October 2017